4-8-0 TENDER LOCOMOTIVES

A Chapelon 4–8–0 of the Paris–Orleans Railway (Cliché SNCF*)*

4-8-0 TENDER LOCOMOTIVES

LOCOMOTIVES

D. ROCK CARLING

DRAKE PUBLISHERS INC NEW YORK

ISBN 87749 150 X

Library of Congress Catalog Card Number
76-175973

Published in 1972 by
DRAKE PUBLISHERS INC
381 Park Avenue South
New York, New York 10016

Printed in Great Britain

CONTENTS

PREFACE

THE 4–8–0 is a type of locomotive that is of quite respectable antiquity, yet is one of those types of steam locomotive that is still at work. It has been used literally 'from China to Peru' and from Norway to Argentina and New Zealand; but it was unknown on the railways of Great Britain, where it was built only to be sent overseas.

This work does not purport to be an exhaustive history of the 4–8–0 type, or to be fully comprehensive: for it to be so would require more extensive research than either the facilities and information available to the author or the time and means at his disposal make practicable.

The subject divides almost naturally into geographical divisions: North America, Europe, Africa, South America, Asia, Australia and New Zealand. North America takes pride of place by virtue of priority in time, the type having originated in the United States and having been built and used there several decades before it was used elsewhere.

There were classes of 4–8–0 that are not recorded here: statistics indicate that only about four-fifths of the engines of this type known to have been built in the USA are included. Because of the differences in construction a clear distinction is made between tender and tank engines. The latter are excluded.

Nomenclature has been used as it was at the time concerned, or at least during most of the period covered. This seems likely to be less confusing than the use of names of countries and railways now current.

The units used in quoting the dimensions of the locomotives are those at present usual in the United Kingdom, most of these being equally valid in the United States and in much of the British Commonwealth.

INTRODUCTION

THE designers and builders of steam locomotives have always imparted much individuality to their products and in this respect the 4–8–0 type is no exception. But there are usually some features common to a number of designs just as a common object has been attained by different means in various countries at various times and on various railways.

If there is one factor that is common to most 4-8-0s it is that they were mountain- or hill-climbing engines. Another is that most of them were built to run over light track, often of mediocre quality, and with sharp curves.

For a locomotive to haul a worthwhile load on a steeply graded line, it must have plenty of weight on its coupled wheels, but if the load permissible on each axle is low, the number of coupled axles must be increased to obtain the necessary adhesive weight. Sharp curves make it desirable for the locomotive to have guiding wheels at its leading end and, if the track is light or of poor quality, a leading bogie is preferable to a two-wheeled truck. Moreover, an engine with a sufficiently large boiler for sustained uphill work may be too heavy to be properly carried by only one carrying axle besides the coupled ones.

The 4–8–0 locomotive meets the requirements just set out in a simple and inexpensive way. In comparison with a 2–8–0 its leading bogie enables a larger boiler to be used for the same axle loads and improves the curving of the engine, but the bogie is more expensive than most two-wheeled leading trucks. Compared to a 2–8–2 it has in its favour that for the same adhesive weight and tractive effort, it is less liable to slip its wheels when pulling hard, but the 2–8–2 allows of more freedom in boiler design, at some extra cost, and of larger coupled wheels without affecting the boiler and so of higher speed if the track will permit.

The conditions mentioned above were met in the United States during the later decades of the nineteenth century and that is where and when the 4–8–0 developed after its first tentative beginnings. There are hills and mountains in plenty and railroad track was comparatively light. Rails are bought by the ton, not by the yard: only after traffic had developed was money available for heavier and better laid track.

The same may be said of railways in Africa, South America, Australasia, and Asia in the last decade of the nineteenth and the first few of the twentieth century. In Europe railways were well established before the 4–8–0 was adopted, but many railways still had light track and in the mountains curvature was often severe. In the British Isles these conditions were generally lacking, railways were relatively strongly built and the fairly short distances favoured the use of more light trains rather than fewer heavy ones. Only on one Irish railway did conditions occur that warranted the use of a 4–8–0, though they almost did so in two cases in England. But more 4–8–0 locomotives were built in Great Britain than in any other country and by seventeen locomotive builders, also more than in any other country, all for export. This British contribution provides an element of unity in design of locomotives for a large number of railways.

A locomotive hauling a load is subjected to weight transfer. This is because it exerts its pull at rail level, but the force to haul the train is applied at the level of the coupling between engine and tender, creating a turning moment, which can only be resisted by the transfer of weight from the front to the back of the engine. For a locomotive with a leading bogie and no trailing truck the effect is to increase the adhesive weight and unload the bogie; even if the leading, or even the first and second, coupled axle is equalised with the bogie the net effect is still an increase in adhesive weight. If the engine has a trailing truck a part of the weight transfer will be to those carrying wheels and the increase of adhesive weight will be less. The whole effect is small but is perceptible and not to be ignored when working near the limit of adhesion.

A similar effect is due to the track being depressed under the locomotive, which alters the loading of the axles, increasing that of those at the ends and decreasing that of those in the middle; again a locomotive with carrying wheels at both ends has its adhesion reduced more than one with a leading truck only. Equalised spring rigging reduces this effect, but does not eliminate it.

The boiler of a 4–8–0 is of simpler shape than that of a 2–8–2 or 4–8–2 and this makes for easier and cheaper boiler making, but, unless the loading gauge is high and the track permits of a high-pitched boiler, the firebox of a 4–8–0 boiler may be unduly shallow if it is wide with its foundation ring above the wheels, or on bar type frames. The ashpan too may be of poor shape, restricting air access to parts of the grate, especially if ash accumulates on an insufficient slope.

The strength of bridges affects the choice of wheel arrangement of a railway's locomotives. It imposes a limit on total weight, weight per unit length, and maximum axle load, the nature of each bridge deciding which is the most severe limitation. If the main restriction is on total weight a 2–8–0 may be more suitable than a 4–8–0, but if it is on axle load the reverse will be the case. Where weight per foot run is the limit the longer engine will be preferable

and some engines have projecting buffer beams and long tenders for this reason.

Added to the technical factors is one which is imponderable but often decisive, namely the opinions of the man in authority, which may be based on experience, prejudice, habit, or even on a single chance incident.

Even the personalities involved may affect the issue. The chief civil engineer may be a stronger personality than the chief mechanical engineer, or of greater seniority; the general manager may have his views or the board of directors theirs.

Lastly comes the factor of cost. The most important aspect of cost may vary from one railway to another and from time to time on the same railway: it may be possible to spend more on new locomotives to secure cheaper operation of the line in the future, or there may be no more money than will buy the cheapest locomotives that will keep the line going.

The play of these factors is mostly hidden in the past, though some may be surmised in certain cases.

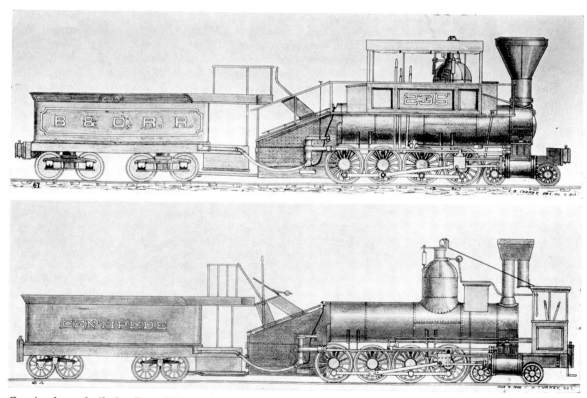

Centipede as built by Ross Winans in 1855 (below) and as modified for use on the Baltimore & Ohio Railroad in 1864 (above). (By courtesy of the Smithsonian Institute. Reproduced from Bulletin 109 of the Railway and Locomotive Historical Society)

CHAPTER 1

NORTH AMERICA

SECTION 1

(a) On American Railways

THE building and operation of railways in the United States is typical of the American way of life: it has always been a matter for private enterprise tempered by state intervention and regulation. Each railway is a separate concern run by individuals in an individual manner. Rivalry was often intense and was reflected in the locomotives.

Many railways were pioneer lines in undeveloped or little developed areas and were built, as such lines usually are, as economically as possible; the line could be improved when the traffic warranted the expenditure. In the early days rails were expensive and of light weight per yard: the track costs far more than the rolling stock, many times more than the locomotives, on most such railways.

The labour originally available for the maintenance and operation of locomotives was rarely highly skilled, so simple robust construction was essential.

With long lengths of single line and few passing places operation of freight trains tends to few heavy trains rather than many light ones, so powerful locomotives were needed, but speed was moderate or low.

The relatively poor track made some sort of leading truck essential for guidance at any but low speed and very early the use of a four-wheeled bogie became customary for most locomotives. The simplicity of the 4–4–0 made it the preferred type for almost all service and only gradually did more coupled wheels become habitual, first for freight and later for passenger trains.

Few railways had facilities for the complete design of locomotives and this work was left to the locomotive builders. Continuity of design was more likely to stem from repeat orders from the same builder than from any other source. Many railways, having found a manufacturer's engines to suit them, obtained most of their requirements from the same source again and again for many years. Others obtained their engines as opportunity offered, influenced by price or quick delivery; urgent need sometimes meant ordering from two or three builders simultaneously.

With so much individuality in design the emphasis in dealing with North American 4–8–0 locomotives is on the increase in size as time went by and on changes of design affecting all steam locomotives such as the increases of boiler pressure.

All this action took place before the backdrop of a vast continent with great mountain ranges, wide plains, though the prairie is by no means flat, and great rivers all in a land that was mainly very sparsely populated.

The story of the American locomotive is very largely the story of America and that of the 4–8–0 is a microcosm of the whole.

(b) Early beginnings

At the very start uncertainty occurs. It has long been believed that the first 4–8–0 locomotive was the *Centipede*, built by Ross Winans in 1855, when it underwent trials on the Baltimore & Ohio Railroad. There is a possibility that a locomotive (1) built in 1844 by the Hinkley Locomotive Works for the Boston & Worcester Railroad *may* have been a 4–8–0; if this could be shown to be so it would make the genesis of the 4–8–0 some eleven years earlier. The point was noticed forty years ago, but the implication seems to have been missed (see bibliography).

Reverting to the *Centipede* (2), for a number of years the Mount Clare shops of the B & O at Baltimore were leased to Ross Winans for commercial locomotive building, the majority of his engines being sold to the B & O, in particular his well-known 'Camels'. Friendly relations had existed between Winans and Samuel Hayes, master of machinery of the railway, but in 1856 Hayes was succeeded by Henry Tyson, a man of strong opinions like Winans himself, but their opinions did not agree and neither was particularly tactful. An acrimonious dispute ensued and Winans refused to sell any more locomotives to the B & O.

Construction of *Centipede* started in 1854 and it was described, still incomplete, in the *Railroad Advocate* of 24 March 1855. Either the paper gave few details or the description became lost. The engine was tested between Baltimore and Washington. It was not until 1863, when Tyson was succeeded by Thatcher Perkins, that matters improved and then the B & O was desperately short of locomotives due to the war between North and South. The B & O was in the zone of hostilities and had lost many locomotives. Winans offered to sell three 'Camels' and *Centipede* and demanded an answer the same afternoon! Such was the B & O's need that he got agreement to his terms. *Centipede* entered service early in 1864 and ran on the B & O for nearly 20 years.

Two reconstructions of this locomotive have been made, due mainly to J. Snowden Bell, a draughtsman at Mount Clare under Thatcher Perkins from 1862 and chief draughtsman from 1865. Writing in 1917 Bell stated that no description or drawings of the locomotive survived and that what little was known depended on '. . . the recollection, naturally dimmed by the lapse of years, of those few now living who, like the writer, have seen the engine'. After his death two sources of information have come to light, confirming Bell's description. The only appreciable discrepancy lies in the drive to the feed pump, which was not as shown in the drawing.

The engine had a number of new features. M. N. Forney, who worked for Winans at the time, stated that these were due to Thomas Winans, one of Ross's two sons, if indeed he did not design the whole engine. The valve gear was remarkable in that two valves were used for each cylinder, a main valve, worked by hook (or gab) motion for reversing and a second cut-off valve, on top of the main valve, worked by a link motion, to permit expansive use of the steam. The bogie had no frames: the two axles were connected to one another by six leaf springs. The bogie centring device was novel, with a roller on inclined planes.

Such was the first 4–8–0 tender engine of which any appreciable record survives; very likely the first of all. This engine was expected to haul the B & O's heaviest passenger trains of the epoch at 20mph up a gradient of 1 in $45\frac{1}{2}$. The dimensions are set out in Table I.

The next appearance of the 4–8–0 type was several years later, about 1869, and it was the result of rebuilding a locomotive of another type; the railway was the Lehigh Valley Railroad, more particularly

Fig 1 *The ninth new 4–8–0 built by the Lehigh Valley Railroad; claimed as the most powerful locomotive in the world in 1880*

14

Fig 2 *An 1881 Rhode Island locomotive for the Atlantic & Pacific Railroad,*
as in use on the Santa Fé many years later

the Beaver Meadow Division of that line. The Lehigh Valley served the Pennsylvania coal fields and ran through some mountainous areas. For a line then concerned mainly in carrying a heavy coal traffic it was severely graded. The Lehigh Valley was progressive in locomotive matters and in 1866 it had acquired the first locomotives built as 2–8–0s and in 1867 the first of the 2–10–0 type. Accounts differ as to which of these was involved in the rebuilding. However it may have been, the rebuilding produced a 4–8–0 (3) that was a success as it was followed a few years later by newly built engines of the same type. If it was originally the *Ant*, one of the 2–10–0s, it had cylinders 20in bore by 26in stroke driving 4ft wheels and the grate area was 28.7sq ft.

The next 4–8–0s were built new in the Weatherly, Pa, workshops of the LVRR, three in 1872 (4) and a fourth in 1873, to the designs of Philip Hofecker, master mechanic of the Beaver Meadow division. They had 20in × 26in cylinders and the coupled wheels of the first three were 4ft 1in diameter and of the fourth 4ft 0in. Another was built in 1878, two in 1879, and one in 1880, all like the 1873 engine.

Then, also in 1880, there was built at Weatherly the famous No 20, *Champion* (5) (Fig 1) designed by Henry Hofecker, by then master mechanic of the Beaver Meadow division, Philip having become master mechanic of the whole railroad. At the time

this locomotive was claimed to be the most powerful in the world.

Weatherly continued to build 4–8–0s at the rate of from one to five a year until 1888 and both Weatherly and South Easton shops rebuilt some, six in 1891 and two in 1892. Twenty-six were definitely built at Weatherly and three of those rebuilt at South Easton did not have their origin recorded, but these also were probably Weatherly built. All had 20in × 26in cylinders, except the last two which had 24in stroke; ten had 4ft 2in coupled wheels and ten 4ft 0in wheels.

These Lehigh Valley locomotives were the true ancestors of the breed in the United States and the 4–8–0 type lasted on the LV until 1917.

In 1881 the Rhode Island Locomotive Works built ten 4–8–0s for the Western Division of the Atlantic & Pacific Railroad. The Western Division of the A & P ran from Albuquerque, New Mexico, to the California boundary at Needles: this was in effect an extension of the Atchison, Topeka & Santa Fé Railroad. From Needles eastward the line rises over 5,000ft to the first summit at an average of 1 in 130 for 125 miles and further on another 50 miles also average 1 in 130 to cross the Arizona Divide at 7,310ft above sea level. These locomotives (6) were Rhode Island's works Nos 993–1002 and originally bore running numbers 26 to 35, later becoming Nos

Fig 3 *The twentieth locomotive and first 4–8–0 built at the Sacramento workshops of the Central Pacific Railroad, claimed in 1882 as the largest locomotive in the world*

237–45 of the AT & SF, one having been scrapped as a result of a boiler explosion in 1887. The last was in service on the Santa Fé in 1924, four having been sold including one to the *Belington & Beaver Creek Railroad* and one, Rhode Island's No 1000 to the Sacramento State Fair Association. Figure 2 shows one of them when owned by the Santa Fé. By then some had migrated further west and were used in the Tehachapi Mountains of California.

The Santa Fé did not have any other 4–8–0s: the even steeper gradients elsewhere induced a preference for 2–8–0, 2–10–0, and 2–10–2s, the last being known as the Santa Fé type. But the Santa Fé did order a 4–8–0 from Schenectady; this was to have been a 'Strong' locomotive with duplex cylindrical fireboxes (6a). This was in the late 1880s or early 1890s. Failure of other 'Strong' locomotives caused the order to be cancelled.

Another specimen of the type then brought the 4–8–0 into greater prominence. For a trunk line the Central Pacific Railroad's main line was very severely graded, crossing the Sierra Nevada mountains at a height of 7,018ft after climbing from 163ft at Roseville in 87 miles, with a ruling grade of 1 in 45½, compensated for curvature, which is sharp and continuous; but there are some pitches at 1 in 37·7.

In 1882 there was built in the railway's shops at Sacramento, California, the 'Enormous' locomotive (7) depicted in Fig 3. This was Sacramento works number 20 and the design was due to A. J. Stevens, the chief master mechanic or locomotive superin-

tendent of the Central Pacific. Again it was the largest and most powerful locomotive in the world. This was the start of the *big power* for which this line has been famous ever since.

So well did this engine perform that twenty-five more were ordered the same year from the Cooke Locomotive and Machine Works, of Paterson, New Jersey. Cooke delivered five of these locomotives (8) in 1882 and the rest in 1883. They were identical with the prototype except for cylinders of 20in bore instead of 19in.

These Stevens engines had two peculiar features, the unusual shape of the firebox and the special steam distribution, that is to say both valves and valve gear. The rear end of the firebox was depressed so that the outer shell was below the water level, leaving no clear steam space. The roof was sloped down towards the back so that steam bubbles would flow forward till they reached the upper vertical part of the backplate which was in two pieces. The firehole door was in the lower backplate. The firebox was very long, 13ft 4¾in to the tubeplate, the grate being 9ft in length. It is not clear what object Stevens had in mind in using this abnormal construction, which must have been costly to build and maintain: it did give more room in the cab.

The special valve gear operated four slide valves for each cylinder, two, one for each end, being worked by Stephenson valve gear, but used for reversing only, and two more, on top of the first two, for controlling the cut-off, these being operated by

16

a third eccentric through a rocking lever with a sliding block on one arm. The use of a double valve gear is reminiscent of *Centipede*, but separate valves for each end of the cylinder were novel on a locomotive. This valve gear gave very good steam distribution even at short cut-offs; short as understood for a saturated-steam engine with a boiler pressure low by modern standards. At long cut-off and a speed of 8mph the indicated mean effective pressure was 124lb/sq in, which is over 91 per cent of the boiler pressure of 135lb/sq in, that is to say more than the 85 per cent normally used to calculate the tractive effort at starting.

In their original condition these engines hauled trains of 395 tons up the long 116ft per mile grades with some lengths of 140ft per mile, at a mean speed of 8mph. [Unless otherwise stated 'ton' means 2,240 lb; a short or US ton=2,000lb and a metric ton, or tonne=2,204·6lb.] One of them, the *Mastodon*, was shown at the Exposition of Railroad Appliances in Chicago in 1883. It was from this engine that the correct generic name of the 4–8–0 type is derived, though the less definite *Twelve Wheeler* may also be used. Though of long standing, the use of the word 'Mastodon' to described the 4–10–0 type is *not* correct.

It was probably the continued good work of this class on the heavy grades and sharp curves of the Sierra Nevada line that caused the 4–8–0 type to be more widely accepted and to be built by several other firms of locomotive builders. In course of time all these engines received new boilers with higher steam pressure, increasing their weights by various differing amounts and they were otherwise modified also, but it is of note that the prototype lasted until it was scrapped in 1935 and two of the Cooke engines were scrapped in 1949 and two more in 1950.

It will now be more convenient to follow the development of the 4–8–0 on each railway in turn rather than sticking to chronological order.

SECTION 2

FURTHER DEVELOPMENT

In 1885 the Central Pacific had become a part of the Southern Pacific Railroad and so it is no surprise to find that railway ordering more 4–8–0 locomotives in 1889. These ten engines were built by the Schenectady Locomotive Works, of Schenectady, NY, and they were little larger than the Stevens engines; they did not have the special features of those locomotives, but the boiler pressure had gone up to 160lb/sq in, which would permit more economical use of the steam in the cylinders (11).

Two years later the Southern Pacific took delivery of the first of a class of two-cylinder Cross com-

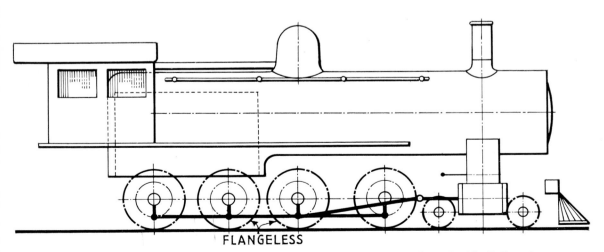

FLANGELESS

Fig 4 *Outline of an 1895 Schenectady locomotive for the Southern Pacific Railroad*

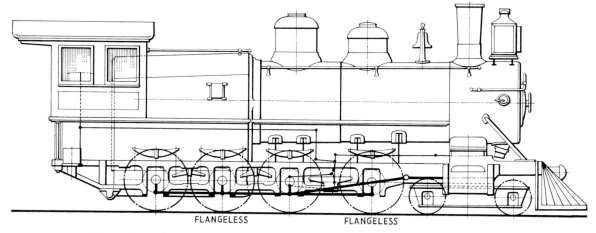

FLANGELESS   FLANGELESS

Fig 5 One of the Great Northern Railway's class G1, built by Brooks in 1891

pound 4–8–0 engines from Schenectady, works No 3547, a dozen more, works Nos 3760-71, following in 1892. These locomotives (12) were, the author believes, the first compound 4–8–0s and compounding, on various systems, enjoyed quite a vogue in the USA for the next decade or so. They had 20in diameter high-pressure and 29in diameter low-pressure cylinders, both with 26in stroke, 180lb/sq in boiler pressure and 4ft 3in diameter coupled wheels. Eight more followed, still in 1892, but with 30in diameter low-pressure cylinders; the Schenectady works numbers followed on immediately after those of the last batch. They were nearly as long-lived as the Stevens class, various dates of scrapping having occurred as late as 1952 and even one in 1954. They had been rebuilt as two-cylinder simples with 20in × 26in cylinders and 170lb/sq in steam pressure.

The Southern Pacific's ever growing traffic over the Sierra Nevada gradients called for more locomotives in 1894, when fourteen heavier 4–8–0s were ordered from Schenectady. These locomotives (19) (Fig 4) were delivered in 1895 and were much larger than either the Stevens engines or any of the previous batches from Schenectady; in a dozen years the engine weight had gone up from 55 to 78 tons and adhesive weight from 47·3 to 65·6 tons, the nominal tractive effort had risen from 23,200 to 35,100lb; simple expansion had been reverted to. They were set to haul trains little heavier than those taken by their predecessors, about 406 tons, but the average speed up the grade had increased from 8 to 12mph, or by 50 per cent. As well as on the Sierra Nevada

line these engines worked in Southern California where the Southern Pacific climbs through the Tehachapi mountains. Several lasted until 1950 and one till 1951 after being rebuilt in 1905.

In 1898 Schenectady was again building 4–8–0s for the Southern Pacific, which had reverted to compounding. There were ten of these two-cylinder engines (26) with cylinders of 23in and 35in bore by 32in stroke. Like the earlier compounds they were rebuilt as simples between 1911 and 1917 and lasted until various dates between 1949 and 1953, except the first, Southern Pacific No 2914, Schenectady works No 4807, which ran until 1955 and is preserved at Bakersfield, California, a partial atonement on the part of the Southern Pacific Railroad for the scrapping in 1935 of the historic No 229 of the Central Pacific. The Southern Pacific sold some of its 4–8–0s to various minor railways, but a number also were transferred, as will be described later, to its subsidiary south of the border. When in California and Oregon in 1927 the author saw some of these old 4–8–0 Southern Pacific engines, but was not able to identify the batches to which any of them originally belonged.

Going back now, it was in 1887 that the Baldwin Locomotive Works of Philadelphia built some 4–8–0 locomotives for the Pennsylvania & New York Railroad, which was, or became, the northern division of the Lehigh Valley RR. More of these engines (9) were built in 1891, by which time there were twenty-five of them, the last ten having somewhat larger boilers.

18

Also in 1887 Schenectady built three 4–8–0s (10) for the Beech Creek Railroad. More followed at intervals of one or two years till there were thirteen by 1891; they were followed in 1893 by eleven more (18) with driving wheels 6in larger and three more in 1897 (25). Finally another five followed in 1898 with wheels 3in smaller. The Beech Creek was situated in the upper valley of the Susquehanna river and gave access to coalfields owned by the New York Central. It was a Vanderbilt road and became part of the New York Central System, all these 4–8–0s passing to the NYCRR. The main line of the NYC is known as 'The water level route', but there are plenty of hills and mountains on either side.

In 1891 Schenectady built two small 4–8–0s for the Fremont, Elkhorn & Missouri Valley RR, one of the then many narrow gauge railways in the USA,

being of 3ft 0in gauge. They were oil burners at one time and also at some period burned coal (13). Another followed in 1892 and in 1902, after the railway had become a part of the Chicago & North Western Railway, two more (41) came from the American Locomotive Company's Schenectady works. It was not unusual for some American railways to change from oil to coal burning and vice versa as the prices of coal and oil varied.

Also in 1891 Brooks built fifteen 4–8–0s for the Great Northern Railway, which were quite an advance on earlier locomotives of the type. A single further one followed in 1893 for the Montana Central Railroad, which became part of the GN; the GN later classified them G1. One of them was Brooks' works No 2000 (14) (Fig 5).

The next American 4–8–0s were appreciably

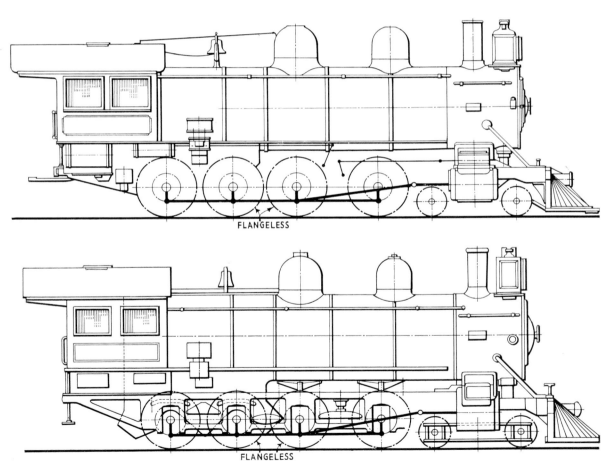

FLANGELESS

FLANGELESS

Fig 6 Schenectady's 4–8–0 locomotives for the Duluth and Iron Range Railway (above) and for the World Columbian Exhibition of 1893 (below)

larger than any, other than the G1s, previously built and a rivalry developed between Schenectady and the Brooks Locomotive Works of Dunkirk, NY, these two builders taking up all the spaces in Table II except one. It may be that other firms built 4–8–0s during the next half-dozen years, but only one class built by Baldwin has been located by the author.

Brooks built one or more engines (15) for the Iron Range & Huron Bay Railway in 1892, a little larger than the GN 4–8–0 of 1891, but very like it. Next year Schenectady built ten a little larger for the Duluth & Iron Range Railway (16) (Fig 6). These two railways were concerned mainly in the transport of iron ore from the immense deposits in the Mesabi, Vermillion, and Iron ranges to the head of Lake Superior for shipment to the iron and steel industry of the USA. The D & IR has become the Duluth, Missabe & Iron Range Railway, but the author has not discovered what has become of the IR & HB. The D & IR climbed rapidly from about 700ft to about 1,650ft in just over fourteen miles, averaging 1 in 80, but the first three miles are at about 1 in 45, a formidable grade even for trains of empty ore wagons; gradients against the loaded trains are less severe but include some four miles averaging 1 in 110.

The D & IR received four more 4–8–0s from Schenectady in 1895 and ten, some in 1896 and some in 1899 (22) (Fig 10) from Baldwin, a little heavier than the 1893 engines.

In 1893 there took place the World Columbian Exhibition in Chicago and both Brooks and Schenectady exhibited locomotives. Amongst these were two 4–8–0s, one by each firm. That by Brooks was for the Great Northern (14) (Fig 5). Schenectady's 4–8–0 exhibit (17) (Fig 6) closely resembled that for the D & IR; was it also for that line or for another?

Brooks built a single 4–8–0 (20) for the St Lawrence & Adirondack RR in May 1896. This bore the name *Manitou* with the running number 15; Brooks' works number was 2667. This railway was a consolidation in that year of an earlier line of the same name, which was located in the Province of Quebec just north of New York State, with the Mohawk & Malone, Malone & St Lawrence, and the Canadian Southwestern. By lease of a branch of the Grand Trunk and running powers over the Canadian Pacific this provided a through route to Montreal. The name suggests penetration into the Adirondack mountains and implies climbing. Whether the 4–8–0 worked in the USA, in Canada, or in both, the author cannot say. In the following year the whole group of lines was leased by the New York Central, which had been behind the whole project. This 4–8–0 was sold in November of the same year to the Buffalo, Rochester & Pittsburgh RR, of which more later.

Meanwhile, still in 1896, Schenectady had built four two-cylinder compound 4–8–0s (21) (Fig 7) to the requirements of E. M. Herr, superintendent of motive power of the Northern Pacific RR. This is a transcontinental line and has to cross the vast mountain barrier commonly thought of as the 'Rockies', but consisting of several ranges. These locomotives had cylinders 23in and 34in bore by 30in stroke and were intended for banking freight trains up seven-

Fig 7 *A two–cylinder compound of 1896 for the Northern Pacific Railroad*

Fig 8 One of class G5 of the Great Northern Railway built by Brooks in 1897 and claimed as the heaviest locomotive in the world

teen miles of 1 in 45½ on the line between Helena, Montana, and Missoula, Montana. On test one of them developed 1,230 indicated horsepower at 112 rpm equal to 18·3mph, a very creditable figure at that date: they had been designed to attain 1,200ihp for three hours continuously. They had one constructional feature of some interest: so large was the low-pressure cylinder that there was no room for the usual flange for bolting the casting to the frame; instead the bolt holes were drilled through into the bore of the cylinder and counter-bored to take the bolt heads, these being covered with Babbitt metal and smoothed off. This was possible in the low-pressure cylinder of a saturated compound without fear of melting the Babbitt metal. These were the first 4–8–0s to weigh over 80 tons without tender.

In December of 1896 the Buffalo, Rochester & Pittsburgh RR placed in service the 4–8–0 it had bought secondhand, giving it the number 139 and name *Mastodon*. It was more appreciated than by its previous owners as it worked on the BR & P till 1918 and three more were ordered from Brooks in 1897 (23), works Nos 2780-2 and BR & P Nos 140-2. The original engine was eventually sold to the Cumberland & Manchester Railroad.

During 1898 Brooks supplied nineteen more 4–8–0s (27) to the BR & P rather smaller than the earlier engines. They had 20in × 26in cylinders, 4ft 7in wheels and a total engine weight of 70·55 tons. Fifteen more followed in 1899. Originally the BR & P used its 4–8–0s for helper service on gradients rarely as steep as 1 in 90, but they enabled the heavy coal trains to maintain uphill the same average speed that the single smaller train engine could achieve on the level. The BR & P grades were severe for a line carrying a heavy mineral traffic. More 4–8–0s, to be mentioned in the next section, came to the BR & P later.

The Butte, Anaconda & Pacific is a short railway in western Montana, not far from the main lines of the Northern Pacific, with a heavy mineral traffic. In 1897 Schenectady built three 4–8–0s (23a) for this line, which were sold in 1917 to the Nashville, Chattanooga & St Louis Railway, after electrification of the BA & P's main line.

In December 1897 Brooks turned out the first two engines of the Great Northern Railway's class G5 (24) (Fig 8), built to the requirements of J. O. Pattee, the superintendent of motive power of the GN, for 'Heavy mountain and pusher service' on 1 in

21

45 grades. The Great Northern and the Northern Pacific were bitter rivals at this time and no doubt Pattee was keen to have a more powerful locomotive than Herr's big compound. Five more G5s followed in 1898 and one was Brooks' 3,000th locomotive. They were claimed once again to be the heaviest locomotives in the world, as they weighed 95 tons without tender, but this distinction was held for only a few months.

The Great Northern obtained another class of 4–8–0 in 1898, also from Brooks, which was for road service, being larger than the G1 but considerably smaller than the G5, with 19in × 32in cylinders and the same boiler pressure and wheel diameter; this G2 (28) was followed in 1900 by the G4 class (37), also from Brooks, which had a slightly larger boiler. Additionally in between the GN obtained some 4–8–0s, later classified G3, from the Rogers Locomotive Works of Paterson, New Jersey (34). All these engines originally had 210lb/sq in steam pressure, but this was later reduced to 180lb/sq in, perhaps due to liability to slipping or to difficulties in boiler maintenance. Some G3s were later superheated and became oil burners (35).

It is now opportune to make a digression about some technical features of the engines and to take stock. One point concerns the position of the driving axle. The drive could be taken on either the second or the third coupled axle, giving rather short or long connecting rods, respectively. A short connecting rod is lighter, but the angularity at mid-stroke is increased: a larger angle means higher thrusts on the slide bars with greater tendency to make the engine pitch and roll. A heavy connecting rod adds to the difficulty of balancing the reciprocating and rotating masses correctly and so increases the dynamic augment on the track: this is not important if speeds are low. Incidentally, balancing of American locomotives was for many years much less sophisticated than it was in Europe. The Baldwin, Brooks and Schenectady engines had the drive on the second coupled axle, but *Centipede* and the Central Pacific ones drove on the third.

Another point concerns the position of the wheels with the blind, flangeless, tyres; all these and most subsequent American 4–8–0 type locomotives had at least one of the coupled axles so fitted and often two. Winans put the blind tyres on the driving and intermediate axles, which was also Schenectady's normal practice; Brooks usually put them on the leading and intermediate axles. No doubt the requirements of the railway sometimes overruled the builder's custom. The Lehigh Valley engines of 1880 had only the second coupled axle with flangeless wheels and the Central Pacific engines had no flanges on the leading and driving wheels. Some of the later Brooks engines had only the leading coupled wheels with blind tyres.

A third point is one that recurs and that affected all locomotives, namely the raising of the boiler to a higher level. In early days it was thought essential to keep down the centre of gravity of the locomotive so boilers were placed as low as practicable, but as they became larger it also became necessary to place them higher above the level of the rails. The process took place partly as a gradual increase and partly as sudden jumps in the height above rail of the centre line of the boiler barrel. For the 4–8–0 type locomotives this dimension was about 6ft 1in in 1880 and 6ft 6in in 1882, but had increased to 8ft 2½in by 1893 and, exceptionally, to 9ft 5in by 1897. Not only had the boilers become larger but the fireboxes were being placed above instead of between the bar frames; the next move would come with the need for still larger grates above the wheels, but that was not yet. With a wide grate extending out sideways there must be enough room above the wheels for a reasonable depth of ashpan; if the slope of the ashpan is too flat the ash will not shake down and will soon restrict the flow of air to the sides of the grate. This is less important for an engine making only short runs if there is time between runs for the side slopes of the ashpan to be cleared. With oil firing, there need be no true ashpan and the problem is eased, but adequate firebox volume is essential.

It is also of interest to note how the number of 4–8–0s had grown, though no exact tally can be given. After a shaky start with perhaps one on the B & W and one definitely on the B & O came a total of 55 on the Lehigh Valley; then 10 on the A & P and 26 on the Central Pacific. Were any built in the interval from 1883 to 1887 exclusive? The Beech Creek had had 32 and the Southern Pacific had received 58 besides those from the Central Pacific. The FE & MV had had 3 to date with 2 more to come: the GN had had 43 also with more to come. The author's information includes no indication of the number of locomotives supplied to the Iron Range & Huron Bay; as this was a line with heavy ore traffic an estimate of about fifteen seems not unreasonable. The BR & P had so far received 23, the Northern Pacific had 4, that have been noted, the BA & P 3 and the D & IR about 19 with more to come. This brings the total to at least 278 and perhaps some twenty more, mentioned above, besides any that have not come to the author's notice.

was a very remarkable locomotive. It was built by Alco for the Delaware & Hudson RR to the requirements of G. S. Edmunds, the superintendent of motive power, and was the fourth of the D & H high-pressure engines.

The D & H had built three high-pressure 2–8–0 locomotives, one each in 1924, 1927, and 1930 with boiler pressures of 350, 400, and 500lb/sq in respectively. All three were two-cylinder compounds. The next development was to a triple-expansion engine, common in marine practice with condensation of the exhaust steam, but very rare for a locomotive exhausting to atmosphere. This involved the use of one high, one intermediate, and two low-pressure cylinders: it was the weight of the additional cylinders that made it necessary to replace the leading pony truck by a bogie. Due to the American dislike of inside cylinders with crank axles all four cylinders were placed outside, the high and intermediate pressure ones at the rear below the cab, and the two large low-pressure ones at the front.

The high-pressure boiler was of the type developed by J. E. Muhlfeld, in which the firebox was replaced by nearly vertical banks of tubes at each side and some nearly horizontal tubes supporting insulation between two steam drums at the top. The grate lay between two water drums at the bottom. There were forward extensions of the upper drums above and to each side of the boiler barrel. The front and back of the firebox were made up of pairs of flat plates with a water space between, stayed in the usual manner. There were six arch tubes. Firing was by a mechanical stoker as was usual in the USA for coal-fired locomotives from the 1920s onwards. These features produced an unusual looking locomotive (45) (Fig 13).

All four cylinders drove the second coupled axle, the two connecting rods being arranged so that one had a forked end embracing the big end of the other. The driving axle was fitted with roller bearings. Poppet valves were used for the steam distribution and were operated by rotary cam gear of the Dabeg type. This gear provided six steps of cut-off in forward gear and three in reverse and a mid-gear position permitting all but the admission valves of the high- and intermediate-pressure cylinders to be held open.

Like most compounds this locomotive had special arrangements for starting so that live steam could be taken direct to both high- and intermediate-pressure cylinders at full pressure and to both low-pressure cylinders at reduced pressure, there being various intercepting valves to prevent flow of steam the wrong way. Thus at least one cylinder at each end would exert a starting effort on the crank. The high- and intermediate-pressure cylinders went into compound working as soon as the pressure built up in the intermediate receiver, but the low-pressure cylinders could be kept working as a simple-expansion engine if the driver so wished. In this way the tractive effort at starting could be raised to 90,000lb as compared to 75,000lb when working on triple-expansion. Normally the change to triple-expansion working would take place automatically after a few revolutions of the wheels, but could be delayed if maximum drawbar pull was needed to accelerate a heavy train. A booster was provided to assist starting and was placed under the tender: this added 18,000lb of tractive effort.

This engine was superheated, whereas all earlier 4–8–0s were built saturated, though some others besides the N & W's 1910 lot may have received superheaters at some time in their lives. The superheater of D & H No 1403 was unusual in that the ends of

Fig 13 *The Delaware & Hudson Railway's high-pressure triple-expansion locomotive No 1403*

the superheater elements projected into the firebox, instead of ending inside the flues some distance from the tubeplate.

The tender was much larger than those of earlier 4–8–0s. It had a four-wheeled bogie at the leading end and a six-wheeled one, which incorporated the booster, at the trailing end.

This engine was the largest and heaviest 4–8–0 ever built, but it was probably not the most powerful (in the true sense of the word, not the common but incorrect use to indicate the greatest tractive effort, regardless of speed). In attaining high power a freight locomotive is at a disadvantage compared with an express engine.

A number of 4–8–0s were built in the USA for export: they will be dealt with in due course.

SECTION 4

THE REST OF NORTH AMERICA

Before leaving North America mention must be made of Canada, Mexico, Cuba and Jamaica.

The greater part of the railway systems of Canada and Mexico form an integral portion of the continental network with through running of vehicles to and from the USA. Cuba could at one time be reached by train ferry so through working of freight wagons was possible there also.

Jamaica is included in North, rather than Central America because of the generally North American attributes of many of its locomotives. The first 4–8–0s for the Jamaican Government Railway were three built in England by Kitson & Co Ltd of Leeds, of basically British design with plate frames. Built in 1901 these standard-gauge engines (46) were small in comparison with those in the USA. Like most American 4–8–0s they had the drive on the second coupled axle and the leading coupled wheels had flangeless tyres; one was tried with the leading coupled wheels flanged and blind tyres on the driving wheels, but the result was unfavourable. In 1914 one was rebuilt with a larger boiler and the other two similarly in 1915 and 1917 (48).

Two engines of increased size were obtained from Baldwin late in 1907 and went into service early in 1908. They were of American design with bar frames and were works Nos 32475–6 (47). The tenders were later enlarged to carry 6¼ tons of coal and 3,500 gallons of water, bringing the total weight to 101·3 tons. The original dimensions are set out in Table IV. The number of boiler tubes was later reduced from 258 to 244, lowering the heating surface to 1,925sq ft.

It was not until 1920 that more 4–8–0s were obtained for the JGR, when seven larger (49) and three smaller (50) locomotives were built by the Canadian Locomotive Company of Kingston, Ontario. The former were for use on the line crossing the very mountainous backbone of the island with long stretches of 1 in 30 and curves of 4 chains (264ft) radius. These locomotives were designed by P. C. Dewhurst, whose name will recur in a later chapter. Typically they had the drive on the third coupled axle, blind tyres on the leading coupled wheels and controlled side play for the trailing coupled axle. The side control of the leading bogie was sufficiently strong to curve the engine with little or no assistance from the flanges of the intermediate coupled axle, which enabled them to run on the four-chain curves at 25mph. They could haul 195 to 205 tons up the 1 in 30 grades at 10mph or 1,740 tons at 15mph on the easy parts of the line. During the second world war six almost identical locomotives (52) were supplied by the same builders in 1944.

The three smaller engines of 1920, though basically similar, differed in several respects from the larger ones.

These Dewhurst locomotives combined features of both American and British practice; they had bar frames. One other 4–8–0 very similar to the Dewhurst engines was built in England in 1936 by Nasmyth Wilson & Co Ltd of Patricroft, Manchester (51) (Fig 14). It was built to the requirements of P. M. McKay.

These Jamaican 4–8–0s also show a steady increase in height of the boiler centre line: it was 7ft 6in in 1901 and 1907, 8ft 3in in 1914, 8ft 9in in 1920, and 9ft 0in in 1935.

The Nasmyth, Wilson engine was involved in a disastrous accident in 1939. A crowded excursion train was being worked by two 4–8–0s, one banking at the rear; between them the two engines were making good time and approached a sharp curve in a cutting at excessive speed. The leading engine and some coaches derailed whilst the banker continued to push; many passengers were killed. This was the first train accident fatal to a passenger on the JGR in 94 years, a remarkable record of safe operation.

Fig 14 *The Jamaican Government Railway's 4–8–0 of 1936, very like the Dewhurst engines of 1920*

The first railway in Cuba was built when the island was still a Spanish possession and, indeed, before the first railway was built in Spain itself. At least three secondhand 4–8–0s from the USA reached Cuba. These were some of the engines acquired by the BR & P in 1900 and 1901 (39) and sold to SI & E in 1919; they were bought, two in the same year and one in 1920 for the Ferrocarril Cubano, which was run by the Hershey interests.

Most railways in Mexico obtained their locomotives from the United States, some new and some secondhand.

The Southern Pacific drew a considerable traffic from Mexico to supplement that arising in the USA and it either assisted local railways in Mexico or developed subsidiary lines. To some of these it transferred locomotives including some of the 4–8–0s. These lines included one with the pleasant name of Cananea, Rio Yaqui & Pacifico: there were copper mines near Cananea. The ultimate subsidiary line was the Sud Pacifico de Mejico, that being correct spelling at the time. Including some via the CRY & P the SP de M had fourteen of the SP's 4–8–0s, all Schenectady built in 1889, 1893, and 1895.

The National Railways of Mexico acquired most of their locomotives from the USA. In general the engines were smaller than their contemporary US equivalents and usually intended for lower speeds. In 1920 they bought secondhand four of the BR & P 4–8–0s of 1897 to 1901.

In 1924 Baldwin built a 4–8–0 for the FCN de M for express passenger service over difficult mountain routes (53). In 1935 five more were built by Baldwin (54) which had slightly larger boilers. These being passenger train engines the coupled wheels were about a foot larger in diameter than those of

the earlier US 4–8–0s, which were for freight service. This larger wheel diameter had one unusual consequence possible only because the locomotives were oil burners: the tops of the trailing coupled wheels were just inside the wide firebox! They were larger and more powerful than any of the US 4–8–0s, with the exception of the D & H triple-expansion engine.

Besides the 4–8–0s for Jamaica, Canada built others for export, but, to the best of the author's belief, the type was never used by any Canadian railway other than the StL & A mentioned above, which was really a part of a US line and on which one 4–8–0 ran for less than a year. Some of those belonging to US railways may have penetrated north of the border.

Conclusion

So the 4–8–0 was built in and for North America over a total period of at least 90 years from 1855 to 1944, and possibly for just over a century. The total number may be estimated at 870 or so and some 40 exported, a total not to be despised even if a small proportion of all the steam locomotives built for North America over the same period. Up to the turn of the century the 4–8–0 did, on four successive occasions, provide a record-breaking locomotive. The steady growth in size is the factor that emerges more than any other from an examination of the tables of dimensions. Clearly this type of locomotive met a definite need for a time on almost all of the many railways concerned, but on each in turn was superseded by other types as conditions changed. In Jamaica they lasted until dieselisation.

CHAPTER 2

EUROPE

SECTION 5

(a) The Background

In Europe the 4–8–0 is less venerable a type of tender engine than it was in North America, but it was built there until more recently and some locomotives of the type are still in service at the time of writing.

Europe takes second place by reason not of strict chronological sequence, but of importance as there were far more 4–8–0s and more classes of them there than in any other part of the world. The first 4–8–0s went into service in Africa, in South America, and in Australasia before any did so in Europe, but the number of engines and of varieties was considerably less. Although one country in Europe is involved far more than any other, there are some dozen countries to deal with, few of them unimportant.

The 4–8–0 type appeared first in Italy in 1902; Ireland in 1905; Spain in 1906, for industrial service; France in 1907; Norway in 1910; Spain in 1912, for main line service; Austria–Hungary in 1915; Poland in 1925; Russia at about the same date; Turkey in 1926; Portugal in 1930; Sweden in 1931. In Belgium, Czechoslovakia, Germany, Great Britain, and Switzerland it was built for export only, though designs for home use were seriously proposed twice in Britain and thrice in Germany. The 4–8–0 was built in Europe for export a decade before it was used at home; the Cape Government Railways imported such locomotives from Scotland in 1892.

There is a doubt about the first 4–8–0 in Europe, as in America. A commentator on the Italian 4–8–0 shown at the Milan Exhibition of 1906, referring to the nearly identical locomotive of 1902, stated that it was the first of the type for standard gauge in Europe. The statement is clear, the implications are not. It could refer to earlier 4–8–0s of standard gauge elsewhere than in Europe, or to an earlier 4–8–0 in Europe not of standard gauge; the author has found no clue to any such locomotive.

Each country is dealt with in turn in the order of the first appearance of the 4–8–0 there with two exceptions: firstly France, where the type appeared a second time after so long an interval that there is little, if any, connection between these events, and secondly Spain, where the story is sufficiently long and complex to fill an entire section.

(b) Italy, Ireland, and Spanish Industry

At the turn of the century the Italian Mediterranean Railway, Rete Mediteranea, was faced with the problem of working increasing traffic up the steep grades of the Giovi line, leading inland from Genoa. The gradient attains a maximum of 1 in 29 and averages 1 in 36 for six miles with a rise of 884ft; tunnels add a further burden. The line is no easy one even to-day with electric traction. The locomotives of this railway have been remarkable from early days and Signor Frescot's No 4501 of 1902 was no exception (55). It was the first of thirty, ten built by Ernesto Breda, SpA of Milan, and twenty by Ansaldo, SA of Sampierdarena, Genoa.

These engines were two-cylinder Cross compounds, the high-pressure cylinder having a piston valve and the low pressure a flat slide valve. The boiler had a wide firebox with the grate above the wheels, 6ft 8½in wide by 9ft 2¼in long, but shallow because the centre line of the boiler barrel was kept down to 8ft 0½in above rail, making the firebox almost of the Wootten shape. The grate of 47·35sq ft did not take up the whole length of the foundation ring as there was a firebrick wall at the front with an ash hopper between it and the tube plate. The RM used the best coal available and had its own fleet

Fig 15 *The Italian State Railways' class 750 of 1906 was almost indistinguishable from the Rete Mediteranea's 4–8–0s of 1902*

of colliers, which plied between Genoa and Cardiff. Italy has to import coal and as costs of transport depend on weight, it pays to buy the best quality.

These 4–8–0s must have been effective as a further ten were built in 1906 by Officine Meccaniche of Milan, usually known as OM; one of these (56) (Fig 15) was shown at the Milan International Exhibition of that year, No 7531 of the newly formed Italian State Railways (FS) works No 78. This batch had slightly longer boiler barrels and were heavier. They were 'coal eaters' and the FS subsequently had them rebuilt with new boilers, which were higher pitched with the centre line at 9ft 2½in above rail. The grate area was reduced, but the total heating surface increased. The rebuilt engines (57) (Fig 16) were more economical and of better appearance. They worked on the southern approach of the Simplon tunnel where the line rises 1,192ft in a little under 12 miles, an average gradient of 1 in 53·3 with a maximum of 1 in 40.

The speed limit fixed for them was 65km/h (40·4 mph) but they were used regularly up to 70km/h and even on occasion at 75km/h (46·6mph). Though used for both passenger and freight traffic, they were mountain rather than mixed traffic engines. All the coupled wheels had flanges and one axle had side play, either the leading or trailing pair. Perhaps the two batches were not alike in this respect, but the rebuilds had the play in the trailing axleboxes. The author may have seen some of these engines at Domodossola in 1914, but he was too young for his recollection to be certain.

It is often not stated whether the values quoted for heating surfaces are measured on the fire or water side; when the data are sufficient the tubular areas quoted are for the water side, converting if necessary. Otherwise a note has been made in the appropriate table. For the firebox the difference is not sufficient to warrant conversion, but for superheating surface it is very considerable.

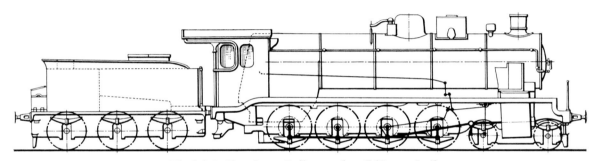

Fig 16 *Italian State Railways class 750 as rebuilt*

Fig 17 *The first class of 4–8–0 locomotives in Spain; one of the second batch for the Compañia Minera de Serra Menera*

The locomotives built for the Londonderry & Lough Swilly Railway in 1905 by Hudswell Clarke & Co Ltd of Leeds, were very different 4–8–0s from those just described. These 3ft-gauge locomotives (58) were more akin to those built for narrow gauge in Africa, Australia, or India than to those for European main lines. They were the only tender engines on any Irish narrow-gauge railway. There were two of them; one ran until 1933 and one till 1953. They were of a simple and straightforward design, with outside frames and outside cylinders, built to the requirements of J. Connor and were for working trains on the 'Burtonport extension'. The line included 4 miles of 1 in 50 gradient. The designed speed was 30mph and coupled wheels of 3ft 9in diameter were provided, the leading pair flangeless. Beyer, Peacock & Co of Gorton, Manchester, prepared an estimate for engines like these in mid 1905, so presumably they put in a tender, but were not successful in obtaining the order. This railway has been well described by E. M. Patterson.

In the following year a Spanish mining concern, the Compañia Minera de Sierra Menera, obtained the first of a series of 4–8–0s, of which a total of sixteen were built between 1906 and 1913 by the North British Locomotive Company. This mineral railway is of metre gauge, but it is more like a main line than an industrial railway; it runs from Sagunto on the Mediterranean coast near Valencia to mines at Teruel, about 85 miles. It crosses the Sierra Menera mountains to reach the mines. To reach the summit at Puerto de Escandon long stretches of 1 in 50 are against both loaded and empty trains, the former needing a banking engine. These locomotives (59) also were more akin to 'Colonial' than to main-line European engines, which is not surprising as North

British and their predecessor companies, Dübs, Neilson Reid, and Sharp Stewart, had been building 4–8–0s for Africa and elsewhere for some fourteen years. They had a maximum axle load of 13·6 tons. The success of the design is attested by the fact that the first nine were followed by five more (Fig 17) in 1907 and two (60) in 1913, NB's works numbers 17401-9, 18093-7, and 20182-3. In the 1950s some were loaned to the FC de La Robla, a public metre-gauge railway in the north of Spain. All were still active at least until the late 1950s.

(c) France, the first period

It was in 1907 that the Chemin de Fer de Paris à Lyon et à la Mediterranée placed in service the first of a class of 4–8–0s intended mainly for goods trains, but used also for passenger trains on difficult routes. The PLM was a large railway and usually did things on a large scale. By 1 October 1910, a total of 185 of the engines (61) (Fig 18) were in service and another 97 on order, making 282 in all, built in the PLM's own works, at Arles and Oullins, and also by the Société Franco-Belge at Raismes, the Société Française de Constructions Mécaniques of Denain, Schneider et Cie (Le Creusot) and the Société de Construction des Locomotives de Battignolles in Paris. They were not all alike as the first series had no brakes on the engine, only on the tender, but those ordered in 1908 had air brakes on the engine. Some boilers had plain tubes and some had serve tubes. As often in Europe some tenders were separately built.

One of the Battignolles engines was shown at the Brussels exhibition of 1910 (62). It was a four-cylinder compound of the type due to Ch. Baudry of the PLM, which had used compounds for many years. In the Baudry system the low-pressure cylinders worked with a fixed running cut-off, which, for these locomotives, was 60 per cent, so that notching up could be done for the valve gear of the high-pressure cylinders only. All originally used saturated steam, but a few were superheated as an experiment in 1909 and many in due course of time (63). Those not superheated were provided with feed-water heaters. On 1 July 1947 the SNCF, of which the PLM had become the Southeast Region, still had 260 in stock.

The design of these engines was initiated under M. Baudry, but he was succeeded by M. Chabal before it was completed. Their speed limit was 85 km/h (52·8mph) and they were expected to haul 1,177 tons on the 'Paris to Marseilles line' at an average of 36km/h (22·4mph), but it is not stated by which route; probably the Bourbonnais line avoiding the steep climbs to Blaisy-Bas. Their axle load being nominally 14½ tons, but in fact 15 tons or a little over, they could run anywhere on the PLM.

A performance recorded by Baron Vuillet may be quoted. Two of these engines, both superheated, hauled a train of 326 tons tare, about 353 tons full, up from La Levade to La Bastide, 31·7 miles averaging 1 in 62, with a rise of 2,694ft, almost the same

as the climb to the St Gotthard tunnel from the south; with a 1 in 40 ruling gradient, 10 chains minimum curve radius and almost continuous 15 chain curves, roughly equivalent to 1 in 36 compensated for curvature, as well as a number of tunnels of small cross section, one 1 mile 125 yards in length. At first, with the engines cold, 18mph was sustained on the 1 in 40, but later 20½mph. The whole climb, including six stops and a signal stop totalling 20¾ minutes, was achieved in 2 hours 1⅔ minutes on a day of storm and rain in August 1928, a running average of 18·8mph.

Reverting to the design features, the inside high-pressure cylinders drove the leading coupled axle and all the coupled wheels had flanged tyres, but side play was provided for the trailing axle. The narrow firebox was deep between the frames, the grate having a slope of 17° down forwards. The boiler centre line was 8ft 6⅜in above rail.

The PLM is known to have prepared a design for a much larger 4–8–0 express locomotive in about 1913 (64) but like many other plans of that time this one came to nothing due to the outbreak of war in 1914.

When the 4–8–0 did reappear in France a quarter of a century after the first of the PLM ones it was much more of an event in the locomotive world: it will be described in due course.

Fig 18 *One of the later batch of* PLM *4–8–0s; the earliest ones had no brakes on the engine, only on the tender* (Cliché SNCF)

4-8-0 TENDER LOCOMOTIVES

SECTION 6

(a) Norway, First Spanish Main Line, and Austria–Hungary

Norway is a sparsely populated country of great distances and is, from the railway point of view, the most mountainous in Europe. Railway construction was of a relatively light character and some of the system was originally narrow gauge, with steep grades and sharp curves. The need for powerful locomotives with low axle loads led to the introduction of the 4–8–0, the first three being built by the Swiss Locomotive & Machine Works, SLM, of Winterthur, in 1910: they were four-cylinder superheated simples with characteristics of their Swiss origin and Norse destination harmoniously combined (65) (Fig 19). All four cylinders were equally inclined and drove the second coupled axle. The two cylinders on each side had one common piston valve so that only two sets of valve gear were required. The use of four cylinders increased the weight, but improved balance permitted a higher speed on light track: the maximum permitted was 75km/h (46·6 mph). The boiler centre line was 8ft 10in above rail.

The Norwegian State Railways, NSB, obtained them partly to work the line between Bergen and Christiania (as the capital was then called), the mountain section of which had only recently been completed. Their intended duty was express trains of about 200 tons up a 2·1 per cent gradient (1 in 47·6) at 35km/h (21¾mph). Much of the Norwegian railway system was then suitable for axle loads of only 12 tons. The summit of the Bergen line is at 4,268ft. The climb from Voss, at 184ft, is made in 43½ miles, 4,084ft rise at an average grade of about

1 in 56, with curves of 820ft radius. The original rails weighed 50lb/yd.

The first three engines were followed by two more, virtually the same, built in Norway by Thune's Mekaniske Verksted, of Oslo, in 1912 (66); they were heavier with nearly a ton more adhesive weight and over a ton extra on the bogie. In 1914 the NSB ordered from Thune's two larger engines with 14 tons axle load (67), these too being four-cylinder simples with the drive on the second coupled axle, still with one valve, of improved design, for each pair of cylinders on one side. The centre line of the boiler was 9ft 6⅛in above rail. All the coupled wheels had flanges and the trailing axle had side play.

These two designs were then modified to make them Woolf compounds with high-pressure cylinders inside and low outside. In this system a single piston valve is used for a pair of cylinders, the high-pressure one exhausting into the same end of the adjacent low-pressure one with no intermediate receiver. The smaller compounds (68), some of which had larger tenders with 5·9 tons and 4,010 gallons, were built from 1919 to 1924 and the larger (69) (Fig 20) from 1921 to 1926. In both cases some were built by Nydqvist och Holm AB, of Trollhättan, Sweden (Nohab) and the smaller ones also by Motala Mekaniska Verkstad, of Motala, Sweden, by SLM again, and the larger by Ernesto Breda of Milan, Italy; both classes also both by Thune, where the design had been carried out, and by the Hamar Jernstöper & Maskinfabrik, of Hamar, Norway.

Fig 19 *Class 26a of the Norwegian State Railways, the lighter four-cylinder simple variety*

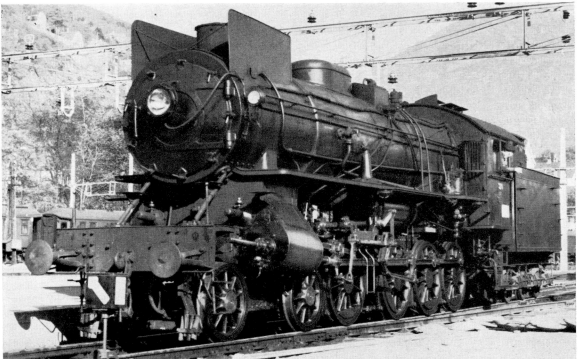

Fig 20 *Class 26c (above) and 31a (below) of the* NSB, *the lighter four-cylinder compound and heavier four-cylinder simple at Otta and at Bergen, respectively, after fitting of smoke deflectors*

Fig 21 *One of the Kaschau–Oderberg Railway's 4–8–0s built by Steg in 1917; except for details like the smokebox door they were almost duplicates of the Südbahn ones of 1915. (Copy of a photograph in possession of the Austrian Railway Museum, Österreichisches Eisenbahnmuseum)*

There were seventeen small and twenty-three large compounds, bringing the NSB total of 4–8–0s to forty-nine. The author travelled behind engines of this sort over the mountain section of the Bergen line in June 1954: the fuel was a mixture of coals from South Wales and Spitzbergen. At Voss it was early summer with flowers and shrubs in bloom, at Finse, just over the summit, winter sports were in full swing.

The 4–8–0s lasted on the NSB until 1965 or later. At some time new boilers carrying 220 and 227lb/sq in were fitted to some of the smaller and larger series, respectively, and one of the former 241. They had formed a major part of the NSB's steam power for four or five decades. Thus in Norway there were two developments that took place in basically similar 4–8–0 locomotives, an increase in power and weight and a change from simple to compound expansion. The Woolf system is not the most efficient or the most effective method of compounding, but is mechanically simple and seems to have given satisfaction on the NSB, where both economy and power output were matters of some concern.

As far as railways are concerned, after Norway, Spain is the most mountainous country in Europe. It was in 1912 that the 4–8–0 type first appeared on the broad-gauge main lines of both the Madrid, Zaragoza & Alicante, MZA, and the Northern, Norte, the two largest railways in Spain. The story of the 4–8–0 in that country is long and complex, covering many varieties of the type, built over the subsequent

forty years. That story will need the whole of a later section so for the present the bare mention of these first two kinds of Spanish main line 4–8–0 must suffice.

The erstwhile Austro–Hungarian empire was also of great extent, mountainous in parts and very early in the field of railway development, but was not particularly wealthy, so the railways were built with light track and bridges and had many steep gradients and sharp curves. Thus again it comes as no surprise that the next appearance of the 4–8–0 in Europe was in the territory of the Dual Monarchy. It was shortly before the outbreak of the first world war that the Imperial & Royal Privileged Southern Railway, Südbahn for short, ordered two 4–8–0s from the State Railway works in Vienna, 'Steg', which built locomotives for other railways besides the State system. They were delivered in 1915 and the first of the pair was Steg's 4,000th locomotive (70).

Intended for use in Carinthia and on the steep climb from Trieste into what is now northern Jugoslavia, they were in fact put to work on the main line over the Semmering pass, with long gradients of 2·8 per cent, 1 in 35·7, and many sharp curves. These were express engines intended for hilly rather than mountain lines and had coupled wheels 5ft 8½in diameter. As the deep firebox was above the wheels the boiler was pitched high with the centre line 10ft 8in above rail. They were two-cylinder simples and were intended to run at 100km/h, 62¼mph, so good balancing was essential. This was a break with Austrian tradition, which had previously favoured four-cylinder compounds for larger locomotives. They were handsome engines with a more modern look than many of their contemporaries. Because of a limitation on length, imposed by the traversers in the workshops, a rather short cab was fitted. One of them was lent to the Kaschau–Oderberg Railway and two years later five very similar engines (71) (Fig 21) were built by Steg for that line, then partly in Austria and partly in Hungary and now in Czechoslovakia. The two towns are also called Kassa and Odra, or Kosice and Bohumin, in the various languages. These locomotives had better cabs than the Südbahn ones and different smokebox doors. The maximum permitted speed was 80km/h. They weighed 84·8 tons, with 59 tons on the coupled wheels, but their tenders carried half a ton less coal and weighed $2\frac{1}{2}$ tons less than the Südbahn ones. Both these classes had eight-wheeled, non-bogie tenders. Side play of an inch either way was allowed for the trailing coupled axle and the tyres on the intermediate wheels had thin flanges. On test one of them hauled 442 tons up 1 in 100 at 31·1mph.

By the time the next development of this class

appeared the war was over, the Austro–Hungarian empire had been dismembered and the main railways in each of the successor states nationalised. After a brief stay in Jugoslavia the Südbahn 4–8–0s were exchanged for 2–10–0s and returned to Austria, but the five Kaschau–Oderberg ones became part of the stock of the ČSD, the Czechoslovakian State Railways.

(b) Austria, Hungary, and Poland

The Austrian Federal Railways, ÖBB, obtained a modernised 4–8–0 from Steg in 1923 (72), the main differences being higher boiler pressure and the use of poppet valves. The maximum permitted speed was 90km/h.

This class was built until by 1928 there were 40 in service. They worked on most Austrian main lines. In recent years many of them were fitted with Giesl 'ejectors' in place of their original blast pipes and chimneys, with benefit to their maximum power output and their economy.

In Austria the earlier 4–8–0s met the requirements well enough for a considerable number of the modernised version to be built.

Fig 22 *Class 11 of the JZ, the Jugoslavian State Railways, are very like the original 1924 locomotives of the MAV, the Hungarian State Railways. (Zagreb, 1968)*

4-8-0 TENDER LOCOMOTIVES

After the second world war the ÖBB lost some of their 4–8–0s to Jugoslavia, where they worked for many years on the Jugoslavian State Railways, JZ, together with a larger number of the next type to be described.

Even in Imperial days Hungary was markedly independent of Austria in locomotive design and construction. The Austrian Südbahn 4–8–0s may have worked into Hungary on the Südbahn and probably did so when lent to the Kaschau–Oderberg Railway, whose own certainly did, but the Royal Hungarian State Railways received twenty-six of their own version of the type from the Royal Hungarian State Iron, Steel and Machinery Works in Budapest in 1924. This was the first batch of a class that was to be built in large numbers by Magyar Allami Vas-, Acel- es Gepgyarak, 'Mavag', as the works became known, not only for the Hungarian State Railways, MAV, but also for export to Slovakia during, and to Russia, Jugoslavia, and China, after the second world war.

Excellent and impressive locomotives they were too, if less handsome than their Austrian fellows. One, built in 1929, was Mavag's 5,000th locomotive. These too were two-cylinder simples (73) (Fig 22).

Between 1940 and 1944, 216 were built for the MAV and 15 for the Slovakian Railways (74) then enforcedly separated from the ČSD. After the war 13 of the MAV engines passed to the JZ as well as 59 newly built ones (75). About 120 were built for the MAV in 1955-6, or thereabouts, bringing the number in service to about 350.

The number delivered to Russia as reparations was probably considerable (eighty is one estimate) and so possibly was the number exported to China. The Chinese may have copied them in their own works. In the mid 1960s some of the Russian ones were sent back to Hungary, displaced in Russia by diesel or electric locomotives. At least it is clear that more of these locomotives were built, between 1924 and about 1956, than of any other class of 4–8–0 and that the MAV had more of one kind of them than any other railway. There were naturally some changes in appearance as this or that fitting was applied or discarded (Fig 23). Two sizes of tender were fitted to them, both bogie tenders with 20 and 24m³ of water, respectively. The trailing axle of these 'Class 424' engines had side play. The maximum permitted speed was 85km/h, commensurate with their 5ft 3¼in coupled wheels. The centre line of the boiler was 10ft 10in above rail, the highest for any standard gauge 4–8–0.

A single design repeated over the years until some 500 or more had been built must have been mechanically sound and operationally suitable for use in several countries. The 4–8–0 wheel arrangement was clearly a good choice in this case. The generous loading gauge allowing a well shaped firebox and

Fig 23 *A later version of* MAV *class 424, with double chimney and smoke deflectors. (Budapest, 1965)*

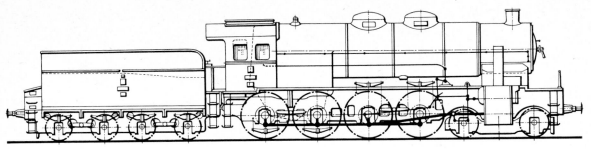

Fig 24 *Class Os24 of the Polish State Railways had a strong resemblance to the Austrian Südbahn 4–8–0s*

ashpan above the wheels had a good deal to do with their success.

The Polish State Railways, PKP, received their first 4–8–0 in 1925 from the 'First Locomotive Works in Poland', Pierwsza Fabryka Lokomotyw w Polsce SA, of Chrzanow, but it was designed in 1924 as indicated by its classification 0s24. The design was based on that of the Austrian Südbahn locomotives, with some features of German Reichsbahn or Prussian State origin, yet the engines as a whole were quite distinctively Polish (76) (Fig 24). Sixty of these

4–8–0s were built by 1926. The larger wheel diameter and higher boiler centre line were due to tyres 5mm thicker than on the Austrian engines.

(c) Russia

The railways of the USSR extend into Asia as well as Europe, but as regards locomotives it is usual to consider them as European; moreover, the engines to be described probably worked more west of the Urals than east of them; at one time the line from

Fig 25 *Class M of the Soviet Railways had several unusual features*

Moscow to Kharkoff was a route where they worked. This design of 4–8–0 tender engine for the SZD was brought out in about 1925 and 'series production' began in 1927. These locomotives (77) (Fig 25) were unusual machines in several respects. They were not a complete success. The man originally responsible, Professor Raevsky, died in 1924; he favoured compounding and perhaps his original project was for a three-cylinder compound, but they were built as three-cylinder simples. It may be added that in Russia, as in Europe generally, it is normal for serving railway officers of high rank to hold teaching appointments, including the tenure of professorial chairs, so a professor may be a practical railwayman rather than an academic theorist.

Though unmistakably Russian, these locomotives give the impression of being at an intermediate stage between the old style and the new. The height of the centre of the boiler barrel is not so noticeable to the eye as that of the Hungarian class 424, perhaps because both the boiler barrel itself and the coupled wheels were larger in diameter; yet the centre line was higher at 11ft 3$\frac{7}{8}$in as against 10ft 10in, though the latter is the second highest for any standard-gauge locomotive in Europe and is the greater of the two in proportion to the gauge of the track. An unusual look is due to the bogie wheels being of unequal sizes, 3ft 5$\frac{5}{8}$in diameter for the leading and 4ft 4in for the trailing ones. The spherical bogie pivot was 2$\frac{7}{8}$in behind the centre of the bogie wheelbase of 8ft 10$\frac{1}{4}$in which would load the trailing axle more heavily, but not so as to require wheels so much larger.

All three cylinders drove the second coupled axle, the wheels of which had flangeless tyres. The inside connecting rod was short and the piston rod so long that it was supported by two crossheads, a small one over the rear axle of the bogie and the main one over the leading coupled axle. Keeping both sets of slide bars in alignment must have been a fitter's nightmare. The inside cylinder was inclined at 1 in 10 on a line starting 4in above the centre of the axle, but there was room for the piston valve to be placed above it in the smokebox saddle. The outside connecting rods were very long, at 11ft 3$\frac{3}{4}$in. The inside valve gear was unusual: it was driven from a second return crank on the left-hand side, this being connected to a rocking lever, transferring the movement inside, the top of which was connected to the *upper* end of the expansion link; another rocking lever was inserted between the end of the radius rod and the top of the combination lever.

These engines, of which about ninety-eight were built between 1927 and 1930, were unsteady in running and were kept to slower trains. There were differences between the first eight engines and those built later; the latter had a wheelbase 7$\frac{1}{2}$in longer and the same total weight, but with about 1$\frac{1}{4}$ tons more on the coupled wheels. The trailing coupled axle had side play. The maximum speed was 90 to 100km/h: test results are quoted up to 100km/h. Some of the engines were oil burners. Later, some, or all, were modified as two-cylinder engines with the boiler pressure raised from 185 to 206lb/sq in (78). This rebuilding was influenced by the fact that at one time over half the engines were out of service with crank-axle trouble.

The SZD had a number of the Polish 4–8–0s, their classification indicating that they were war booty; they would have been converted from standard to 5ft gauge and fitted with automatic centre couplers. The SZD had some Hungarian 4–8–0s (73) built new by Mavag, in about 1946 to 1948, and some of them later returned to Hungary converted from broad to 4ft 8$\frac{1}{2}$in gauge and fitted with side buffers and screw couplings.

SECTION 7

(a) Turkey, Portugal, and Sweden

Turkey is another mountainous land of great distances and is included here as Turkish locomotives are more European than Asiatic. The thirteen 4–8–0s built for the Turkish State Railways, TCDD, in 1926 by Henschel & Sohn, of Kassel, were German in character, many details being Prussian State Railways or Reichsbahn items. The Prussian State Railways prepared preliminary designs for a 4–8–0 version of the well-known P8 4–6–0 mixed traffic engine, with the axle load reduced from 17$\frac{1}{2}$ to 14 tons and the coupled wheel diameter from 5ft 9in to 4ft 7in. The Turkish engines (79) (Fig 26) were also derived from the P8. They were for expresses between Haidar Pasha and Ankara and went into service early in 1927: later they were used on suburban trains and in 1968 some were acting as assisting engines in European Turkey. A dozen similar engines (80) came from Henschel and Krupp be-

Fig 26 *One of the later series of Turkish State Railways 4–8–0s*

tween 1932 and 1934. They were fitted with a counter-pressure brake, useful in mountainous country provided the drivers have been trained to use it correctly. Some were in service at the time of writing. They were rated to haul 315 tons up 1 in 66·67 at 21¾mph and could traverse curves of 590ft radius. The trailing axle had side play. The boiler centre line was 9ft 6⅛in above rail. The second batch had larger tenders. Some worked in the extreme south of Turkey and were used on the Taurus Express.

Portugal was later than her larger neighbour in introducing the 4–8–0 to her railways, but in 1930 did so with some remarkable engines. The small Beira Alta Railway formed part of the route from Lisbon to Paris and of one of two routes from Lisbon to Madrid. It is steeply graded and lightly constructed. Powerful locomotives of light weight were needed. Henschel & Sohn built three four-cylinder de Glehn compound 4–8–0s with bar frames (81) (Fig 27). The drive was divided, the outside high-pressure cylinders driving the second coupled axle and the inside low-pressure ones the leading coupled axle, but the cylinders were in line, not staggered with the inside cylinders well forward of the outside ones. The firebox was above the frames so the boiler

was pitched high, the centre line being at 10ft 2in above rail. The wheels of the second coupled axle had thin flanges and the trailing coupled axle ⅜in side play either way. They were both efficient and effective engines. They used to work the Lisbon portion of the Sud Express from Pampilhosa up to the Spanish frontier at Vilar Formoso, 125½ miles mostly of climbing, in 232min, with seven stops, about 32½mph average. The summit at Guarda is 2,438ft higher than Pampilhosa, the distance being 97 miles. The original stipulation was to climb from Gouveia to Guarda at 65km/h, 40·4mph, with 236 tons start to stop; the distance is 38⅜ miles and the rise about 1,440ft, with a downhill start for a couple of miles and then an almost unbroken climb averaging 1 in 125 with maximum grades of 1 in 67. On an early run one of them took up 234 tons at 43·6mph. The authorised maximum speed was 90km/h. The Beira Alta was eventually absorbed by the CP, the Portuguese Railway Company, and these locomotives were taken into the CP stock.

The CP also had half a dozen two-cylinder simple 4–8–0s built in Spain. Two of these were built by La Maquinista Terrestre y Maritima, of Barcelona, in 1945; two more came from Macosa, formerly

Fig 27 *One of the Beira Alta Railway's four-cylinder compound 4–8–0s, when in*
CP *ownership; the smoke deflectors are a later addition*

Fig 28 *The Swedish State Railways class E10 were still in service in 1970. The similar*
Halmstad–Naessjo Railway locomotives became SJ *class E9. (Östersund, 1969)*

Devis, of Valencia, in about 1947. They were almost the same as some built for the MZA and for the Oeste in Spain. The Portuguese engines (82) were driven from the opposite side of the cab, but were essentially Spanish. What firm built the other two is not known to the author.

There used to be many private railways in Sweden besides the main State system. Amongst them was the Halmstad–Naessjo, a busy line of light construction. In 1931 three 4–8–0s were built for the HNJ by Nohab, which were good examples of Swedish locomotive design (83). They were light but powerful with a maximum axle load of 13 metric tons, being three-cylinder simples. Three more were built by Nohab in 1937. The HNJ was later absorbed by the SJ, the Swedish State Railways, which thus acquired its first 4–8–0s, but in 1947 the SJ needed some good, modern, lightweight steam locomotives and ordered ten similar to the Halmstad–Naessjo ones, the engines from Nohab and the tenders from Vagn & Maskinfabriks AB, of Falun (84) (Fig 28). They were the last steam tender engines to be built for the SJ. The axle load was reduced to $12\frac{1}{2}$ metric tons by moving the boilers forward a few centimetres.

(b) France : the Chapelon engines

Returning now to France, which was left in 1910 with the PLM 4–8–0s of 1907 being multiplied in large numbers, the story can be resumed.

At the start of the 1930s people concerned with locomotives, both professionals and amateurs, were awakened to something tremendous happening on the Paris–Orleans Railway: astonishing performances were being put up by old Pacific locomotives that had been rebuilt according to the precepts and designs of André Chapelon. Never before had such feats of haulage been achieved by engines of so limited a size, yet even these feats were soon to be excelled. On 16 August 1932 another 'Rebuilt Pacific' was steamed for the first time at the Tours works of the PO; No 4521, which had been more radically altered and converted into a 4–8–0. So well did this engine (85) perform that a further eleven were rebuilt, Nos 4702-12 (the prototype was renumbered 4701), emerging from Tours works between February and May 1934. The production batch (86) (*frontispiece*) differed only very slightly from the first engine. So numerous were their outstanding feats that only a few can be briefly quoted.

With twenty-two coaches weighing 1,006 tons one was set to run from Bordeaux to Angoulême in the timing of the Sud Express, then the fastest long-distance train in Europe and generally loading to about 300 tons. This task was successfully accomplished.

On the Nord a train of 636 tons was worked from Paris to Calais at a mean running speed of 73·9mph with a stop at Amiens; an average of 87mph with peaks of 92 was sustained from Amiens to Etaples. With 640 tons $102\frac{1}{4}$ miles from Calais to Amiens, with a steep climb at the start, were covered at 73·6 mph. Restarting, the run to Paris was made at an average of 77·8mph for the 78·6 miles, again starting uphill. The mean drawbar horsepower was 2,000.

On the Central France line, with long 1 in 100 grades they enabled the loading of passenger trains to be increased by about 40 per cent and the timings to be cut by an hour or more simultaneously.

They regularly performed feats that were rarely, if ever, attainable with other engines; when driven hard and skilfully, and vigorously fired, their peak performances were without parallel.

The following anecdote illustrates the spirit in which the crews went about their jobs. A semi-fast for Bordeaux left Angoulême 28min late behind a rebuilt Pacific. The train of eighteen vehicles weighed 806 tons; driver Maillebuau merely said to his fireman 'Il faut travailler' ('we've got to work'). Despite loss of time at two stops due to drawing up, 15min were recouped in the 84 miles to Bordeaux.

The 4–8–0s and rebuilt Pacifics were lent to other French railways and outdid the best that any of their locomotives could do, fine engines though they were. This aroused much admiration and, not unnaturally, a good deal of jealousy also, not only in France.

A further twenty-five were rebuilt at Tours in the difficult years 1940 to 1942, for the Southeastern Region of the SNCF, the former PLM. They were fitted with mechanical stokers, but lack of supply prevented the fitting of roller bearings to the axleboxes of the heavily loaded bogie. These locomotives (87) (Fig 29) had much larger tenders than the earlier ones, which had used a Nord tender for long non-stop runs off the PO. Their work was so good that the building of twenty-five new engines was authorised by the SNCF, but prevented by war and occupation by the enemy.

One of the later engines on test worked a train of some 787 tons from Les Laumes to Blaisy-Bas summit, 19·4 miles, at an average of 66·6mph with a mean of 3,145 drawbar horsepower. That the 1907 PLM 4–8–0s hauled 830 tons up the final length of 1 in 125 at 15mph is some measure of the progress in steam locomotive design.

The characteristics to be noted were the long,

43

Fig 29 *Class 240P of the* SNCF

deep, narrow firebox fitted with a single thermic siphon and a grate inclined more steeply at the front to facilitate hand firing; the high degree of super-heat obtained with the Houlet superheater; four-cylinder compound machinery, on the du Bousquet-de Glehn system, with high- and low-pressure cylinders proportioned for equality of power output and controlled by poppet valves; amply sized steam passages; the double 'Kylchap' exhaust system, which enabled very high rates of combustion and evaporation to be achieved without excessive back pressure in the low-pressure cylinders; the high, but not too high, boiler pressure. The boiler centre line was 9ft 4¼in above rail, a measure of the smaller French loading gauge compared with those farther east, and was adequate with the firebox between the frames.

Younger readers may be referred to the technical and semi-technical publications listed in the bibliography that cover these engines and their feats.

As long as these locomotives received proper attention and good lubricating oil they were trouble-free in service, judged by a very high standard. During the second world war, when they were set to work trains of 1,250 tons and more with inadequate maintenance and inferior oil there was an abnormal failure rate in service: many of the failures were due to hot bogie axleboxes. Some reports of low mileages and poor availability for these engines do *not* bear critical examination. Did not express locomotives, including some of the finest, in Britain and elsewhere in similar, but less arduous, circumstances give unwonted mechanical trouble?

As hostilities drew to a close most of these 4–8–0s were drafted to the Northern Region of the SNCF due to the imperative need to move heavy coal trains from the coalfields to the Paris region. Many years before tests on the Est had shown that these 4–8–0

express engines were capable of, and suitable for, heavy freight haulage. There were not enough serviceable freight locomotives available.

These were indeed the most magnificent examples of the 4–8–0 type, masterly locomotives designed by a great master of his craft.

(c) A Model and some 'Might-have-beens'

No 4–8–0 tender engine ever worked on the public railways of Great Britain; that country's contribution is none the less large, in the form of the great number of 4–8–0s built for export. Most of the countries building locomotives for export did build some 4–8–0s, but none on such a scale as Great Britain. Almost all the 4–8–0s for Africa and Asia, many for South America, and some for Australia and New Zealand were of British manufacture. Seventeen firms of locomotive builders participated in this effort.

Nevertheless one 4–8–0 has hauled passengers in Britain, J. C. Crebbin's remarkable *Sir Felix Pole* (88) (Fig 30). Built to a scale of ¾in to the foot, on 3½in gauge, it pulled trains carrying up to fourteen passengers at the *Model Engineer* exhibitions of 1926 and 1927 and elsewhere. It had cylinders 1 1/16in and 1½in bore by 1⅝in stroke and coupled wheels 4⅞in diameter, equivalent to full-scale sizes of 17in and 24in × 26in and 6ft 6in wheels; steam pressure was 100lb/sq in, not a scaleable value.

There were two projects for full size 4–8–0s in Great Britain, on the London Midland & Scottish Railway and on the Southern Railway. On the former, as related by E. S. Cox, H. P. M. Beames, last CME of the London & North Western Railway and then mechanical engineer, Crewe, put forward a proposal for a large 4–8–0 goods locomotive,

Fig 30 *What a British 4–8–0 might have been like*: *J. C. Crebbin's*
$3\frac{1}{2}in$ *gauge* Sir Felix Pole

having the boiler of the enlarged Claughton 4–6–0 express engine and two outside cylinders. The proposal (89) was not adopted. On the Southern, amongst designs for standard locomotives prepared by the CME, R. E. L. Maunsell, was a 4–8–0 for heavy goods trains. The traffic in mind was coal from Kent, but because of the intense passenger services such trains would need to move fast, for mineral traffic, from one yard or loop to another. The design project was for a four-cylinder simple (90) (Fig 31) which would have been an eight-coupled version of the *Lord Nelson* 4–6–0 express engines with smaller coupled wheels, the same boiler and cylinders with pressure reduced to keep the tractive effort commensurate with the adhesive weight.

The objection was not to the locomotive, but that heavy expenditure would have been incurred in lengthening passing loops if trains were to be operated heavy enough for the project to be economic. Circumstances changed, the traffic did not arise and the engines were not built. Such might have been a British 4–8–0.

There were also suggestions for possible 4–8–0s for Great Britain by various engineers privately. One was for a six-cylinder compound with two high- and four low-pressure cylinders, described in the *Locomotive Magazine* for November, 1945, by J. M. Doherty: the object of having four low-pressure cylinders was to keep within the narrow British loading gauge (90a) (Fig 32).

In Germany preliminary designs for 4–8–0s for home use were twice worked out and another proposal was discussed by the responsible authorities. The first design (91) was before the first world war, as mentioned when describing the Turkish 4–8–0s. The proposal for an experimental locomotive in 1934 was stimulated, no doubt, by the performance of the Chapelon engines. There was then controversy about how to get a larger ratio of firebox volume to grate area on German locomotives, as the authorities then had a dislike of combustion chambers. The idea was dropped, but not before two senior officers of the Deutsche Reichsbahn had witnessed dynamometer car trials of a Chapelon 4–8–0 between Paris and Cherbourg on the Etat. This engine would have been an express locomotive (92) with 18 metric tons axle load and 6ft $6\frac{3}{4}in$ diameter coupled wheels.

The second design was prepared when an express engine more powerful than the 01 class Pacific was being discussed. The Borsig Locomotive Works, of Tegel, Berlin, proposed a 4–8–0 with 20 tons axle load (93), but a larger engine was built, the 06 4–8–4. One reason for rejecting the 4–8–0 was that the long narrow firebox would have caused difficulties in workshops not tooled to deal with it; another was that there was a requirement for the engines to work for a time on routes where the permitted axle load was still 18 tons; the reduction could be made by transferring weight from coupled to carrying wheels, but only with carrying wheels at both ends, which excluded a 4–8–0.

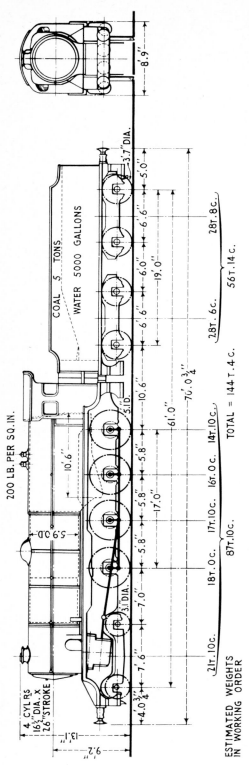

Fig 31 *R. E. L. Maunsell's design for a mixed-traffic 4–8–0 for the Southern Railway*

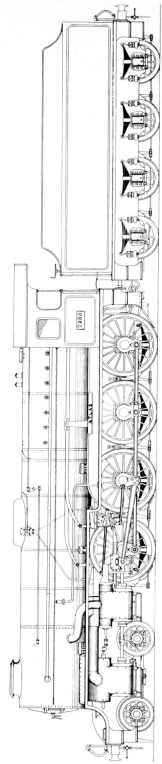

Fig 32 *J. M. Doherty's proposal for a British six-cylinder compound 4–8–0*

SECTION 8

SPAIN

Spain is a very mountainous country and as its railways had to be built cheaply the proportion of steeply graded track is higher than in most European countries.

There used to be a number of private railway companies, two large, one of medium size, a number of small, and a lot of local ones. The large ones were the Madrid, Saragossa & Alicante, MZA, and the Northern, *Norte* in Spanish.

The first two 4–8–0s mentioned in Section 6 (a) were classes 1100 of the MZA and 4000 of the Norte.

The engines of class 1100, for mixed traffic, were two-cylinder superheated simples with moderate sized coupled wheels; the first few were delivered in 1912 and all ninety-five by the following year by Henschel & Sohn. This was the largest single order placed with a locomotive builder in Europe at one time till then. In ordering locomotives the MZA was like the PLM, usually doing things in a big way. These engines (94) (Fig 33) were to haul 345 tons up 15 per mille, 1 in 66·67, at 18½mph, a performance that they bettered by some 40 per cent. This was the forerunner of a succession of classes of 4–8–0s on the MZA; Henschel supplied twenty-five more in 1921.

The Norte main line is the Spanish part of the route from Paris to Madrid and has some formidable gradients. From 16ft at San Sebastian it rises 2,182ft in about 50½ miles to Cegama summit with an abrupt drop of 450ft in about 3·7 miles to Alsasua. The level then varies between 2,980ft at Quintanapalla, 1,515ft at Miranda de Ebro, and 2,800ft at Burgos, 103 miles from Alsasua; then some ups and downs to Medina del Campo at 2,370ft in another 155½ miles. The climb over the Sierra de Guadarrama, via Avila, 3,710ft, reaches the summit, La Cañada, at 4,460ft, then down to 3,020ft at El Escorial and 1,935ft at Madrid Norte, 128 miles from Medina. The line between Medina and Madrid has long 1 in 55½ and short 1 in 48½ gradients amongst windswept mountains subject to violent storms of rain and snow. The winter temperature at Avila sometimes drops to –20°C, 36°F of frost.

Working the heavier trains over this route has always been difficult and it was for this purpose that the Norte acquired six 4–8–0s in 1912 and fourteen more in 1914; they were four-cylinder superheated compounds on the de Glehn-du Bousquet system and had fairly large coupled wheels. All were built by the Société Alsacienne de Constructions Méca-

Fig 33 *Ex-*MZA *class 1100 No 240.2162. (Caceres, 1963)*

niques, SACM (95) (Fig 34). Twenty-five more were built by Henschel in 1921. The class was long lived, as also were the MZA 1100s, some of each lasting into the later 1960s.

It will now be easier to follow events on each railway in turn.

The Norte's next class of 4–8–0s had an unusual inception. In 1921 the Sociedad Española de Construcciones Babcock & Wilcox, of Bilbao, took up locomotive manufacture and ordered one 4–8–0 three-cylinder simple from the Yorkshire Engine Company, of Sheffield. This prototype was to suit the loading gauges of both Norte and MZA, one being wider and the other higher; it was built in 1922 (96) and served as a model for fifteen similar ones built by B & W in 1923. All were purchased by the Norte and classified 4300; they worked until the early 1960s. Three-cylinder engines were something of a rarity in Spain. They had trapezoidal grates like the earlier Norte compounds. Trapezoidal grates had been introduced for some Pacifics of the Paris–Orleans Railway and were more often applied to locomotives with trailing trucks, but also above moderate sized coupled wheels, if the boiler centre line could be high. For a given grate area it was easier to apply such a grate on a broad-gauge loco-

motive, as it was wide at the back, above the wheels and narrow at the front, between the frames with an adequate depth of firebox and a suitable slope for the grate. The valve of the inside cylinder was worked by a conjugated mechanism from the valve gears of the outside cylinders; the inside cylinder drove the leading coupled axle and those outside the second.

The Norte had no more 4–8–0s for the rest of its separate existence, but other 4–8–0s came to its lines after nationalisation.

On the MZA the 4–8–0 went from strength to strength. Immediately after the first batch of class 1100 a new class was ordered, more powerful and intended for passenger and fast goods trains. These class 1300 engines (97) were built by the Hanover Machine Works, 'Hanomag'; eight were ordered in 1914, seven being delivered that year and one in 1920. They were four-cylinder compounds with larger coupled wheels than the 1100s. More were soon wanted, but as none could be obtained in Europe during the first world war twenty-five were built to the German drawings by Alco in 1916 (98) (Fig 35). They were larger than the 1912 Norte compounds and all four cylinders were in line, not staggered. The inside cylinders were appreciably in-

Fig 34 *Ex–Norte four-cylinder compound No 240.4002. (Castejon, October 1963)*

Fig 35 *Ex-*MZA *four-cylinder compound 1300 class No 240.4055.*

clined. There were only two sets of valve gear, a common piston valve controlling both cylinders on one side: they were Woolf compounds. The Alco ones had 214lb/sq in boiler pressure instead of 221 for the Hanomag engines. The original specification stipulated the haulage of 275 tons up 1 in 66·67 at 31mph, 305 tons up 1 in 100 at 37mph, and 335 tons on the level at 62mph.

In 1920 also the new San Andres works of La Maquinista Terestre y Maritima, MTM, of Barcelona, started production of class 1400 4–8–0s for the MZA, the first having been built in 1918, these engines (99) (Fig 36) being two-cylinder simples generally like the 1100s, but with the larger coupled wheels of the 1300s and of much the same size. So successful were they that the MZA continued to obtain them from MTM in all but two of the next eleven years, with modifications in course of time, such as Lentz and Dabeg poppet valves and valve gears for the later ones, five with the former and sixty with the latter. One of the 1100s had earlier been converted from piston to Lentz valves and valve gear with satisfactory results. There were five different total weights of engine and tender, from 140·15 to 145·05 tons. The first change came in 1926 after fifty had been built in four years, a second

Fig 36 *One of the later* MZA *class 1400 4–8–0s*

D

Fig 37 *Ex-Andaluces class 400 No 240.2049, one of the German-built engines.*
(*Cordoba, October 1963*)

in 1928 after twenty-five more, a third in 1929 after another thirty, and a fourth in 1930 after another thirty. A final thirty took just over a year to complete, making a total of 165. The differences of weight were due party to application of various forms of feed-water heaters. The original engines hauled 500 tons on most main lines of the Catalonian division of the MZA, the fast freights of 335 tons at 50mph on the level and up 1 in 66·67 for six miles from Mora to Argentera at 28mph. Some of them were later equipped for oil burning and 75 so fitted were in service in 1969.

In 1936, the MZA obtained ten 4–8–0s from MTM (100) like the 1400s all with Lentz valve gear and poppet valves and with larger tenders. Ten more were built by MTM in 1940. They had large smoke deflector screens and the footplating at the front sloped up to the smokebox like some of the British Railways standard locomotives. These, MZA class 1360, were also working in the late 1960s.

After the civil war in Spain the primary need was heavy repairs of many war damaged, over-worked and under-maintained locomotives; few new ones could be built at first. The outbreak of the second world war made things more difficult, in particular preventing import of copper firebox plates so that steel had to be used and the Spanish steel industry

had to acquire the technique of making the special quality of steel required.

The MZA's last order for 4–8–0s was not all delivered until after nationalisation, fifty from MTM and twenty from the Compañia Euskalduna de Construccion y Reparacion de Buques, which had started locomotive building at Bilbao in 1924.

In 1914 the Andalusian Railways, Ferrocarriles Andaluces, ordered fifteen lightweight 4–8–0s from the Société Franco-Belge, of La Croyère, Belgium; they were delivered in 1920 and were two-cylinder simples (101). More were ordered in Germany in 1921; ten from the Berlin Machine Works (formerly L. Schwartzkopff), one built in 1921 and nine in 1923; fifteen from Borsig, built in 1922; and ten by Hanomag in 1922, works Nos 9779-88, making fifty in all.

The original engines had six-wheeled tenders, the later ones (102) (Fig 37) bogie tenders. With 13 metric tons axle load and low weight per foot run they suited the light track and bridges of limited strength, but the wheelbase was long for the sharp curves even with side play in the trailing axleboxes. Unlike most Spanish 4–8–0s they had narrow fireboxes between the frames.

These Andaluces class 400s were rated to take 180 tons up a 3 per cent gradient, 1 in 33.33, at $15\frac{1}{2}$

mph, 250 tons up 1·5 per cent at 31mph and 330 tons up 1 in 200 at 43½mph, but one of them was observed by Baron Vuillet to take a mixed train of 510 tons from Alhondiguillo to El Vacar Villaharda with 4½ miles of 1 in 50 uncompensated for curvature at a mean speed of 9·3mph despite nearly stalling more than once. In northern Spain the adhesion would rarely have been sufficient for an engine with only 49 tons adhesive weight to haul such a load up the equivalent of about 1 in 46 compensated. Adhesion is better in the south than the north where, to make things worse, the wind is often strong enough to make sanding inadvisable or ineffective.

A heavier 4–8–0 class was put into service by the Andalusian in 1926, with smaller coupled wheels and a shorter wheelbase (103). Ten were built by MTM and ten more in 1927. This was a successful design and a further fifteen (104) (Fig 38) were built in 1942 by Construcciones Devis SA of Valencia. These were Andaluces class 4200, an appreciable advance on class 400 thanks to easing of weight restrictions.

In 1935 the Andalusian introduced some larger 4–8–0s, class 4250, built by MTM. These locomotives (105) were the basis for the later 2400 class built in large numbers after the end of the civil war. Their greater size shows that some of the Andalusian's track and bridges must have been upgraded. They were the last 4–8–0s for the Andalusian before nationalisation.

A small railway, the Medina del Campo–Zamora y Orense–Vigo, obtained four 4–8–0s from Linke Hofmann Werke, of Breslau, in 1922 (106). After it amalgamated with others to form the Oeste, the Western Railway, four (107) were built in 1928-9 and four more, slightly heavier, in 1931 by Euskalduna (108) (Fig 39).

The next variety of 4–8–0 was built for the Oeste in 1932 by Euskalduna and B & W, who supplied five each (109) (110) (Fig 48). They were larger than before and were Oeste class 1000. The Oeste ordered all over Spain for in 1933 five came from Devis (111), in 1934 five from B & W, four from MTM (112) and four from Euskalduna, then two more from Devis in 1935; a final batch of eight came from Devis in 1940. Like many Spanish locomotives of the period they had feed-water heaters.

Some engines of all the last six classes mentioned worked until the 1960s.

The Oeste's final order for 4–8–0s was for a modified version of Andaluces class 4250 and they were delivered in 1942 after nationalisation.

The Central of Aragon was a small, progressive railway, largely Belgian financed. In 1927 the C OF A obtained four 4–8–0 express engines from Les Ateliers Metallurgiques, of Tubize, Belgium (113) (Fig 40). They had coupled wheels of larger diameter than any previous Spanish 4–8–0s, equal to those of the Polish 0s24 and fractionally larger than those of the Mexican 4–8–0 of 1924 and the Austrian ones of 1915. They worked the C OF A's expresses over a route with 1 in 46·5 gradients until the opening four

Fig 38 *Ex–Andaluces class 4200 No 240.2446. (Ronda, March 1966)*

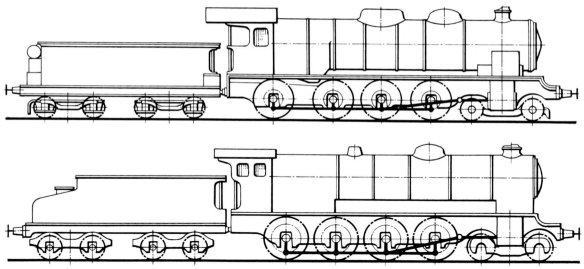

Fig 39 *Oeste classes 830 (below) and 1000 (above); the 1000s differed only slightly from the* MZA *1400s and the* CP's *Spanish-built 4–8–0s were a later version of them, with smoke deflectors*

years later of the direct line from Caminreal to Saragossa, when much heavier expresses to and from Valencia were hauled by 4–6–2 + 2–6–4 Garratts. The C OF A main line partly parallels the Sierra Menera mineral railway (Section 5 (b)), but, being built later, it had to be more steeply graded: the narrow-gauge line already occupied the best location.

Some 4–8–0s had been ordered after the civil war

by both the Oeste and the MZA; the first were completed by MTM in 1940. Five were for the Oeste, and seventy for the MZA, both classifying them as '2400'; so Nos 2401-5 were applied to similar locomotives on each railway. By the time all were delivered the Spanish broad-gauge main lines had been amalgamated into the Red Nacional de los Ferrocarriles Espanoles, RENFE.

The Oeste engines (114), RENFE Nos 2471-5, had

Fig 40 *Ex–Central of Aragon No 240.2072. (Teruel, March 1965)*

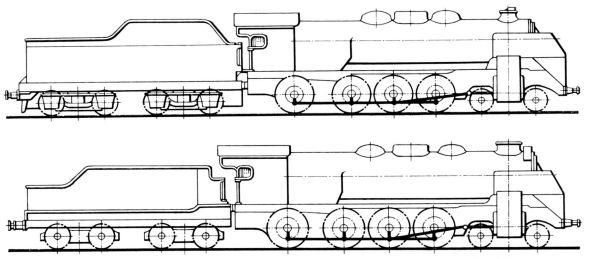

Fig 41 *Two versions of the Renfe's 2400 class: (above) one of those ordered by the MZA, (below) a later variety with double chimney*

larger tenders than the Andaluces 4–8–0s and other changes raising the weight by 17 tons. The MZA ones, of which 23 were delivered in 1942 and 27 in 1943 and 1944 by MTM (115), and 20 in 1943 by Euskalduna (116) (Fig 41), RENFE Nos 2481-550, were heavier again by 6·6 tons. The gap in the RENFE numbers was filled by the Andalusian engines.

The RENFE continued to order engines of this class with modifications for many years. Some were built as oil-burners and the rest later converted to burn oil. This class (117) (Fig 41) was built by all the above-named Spanish builders from 1944 until 1953 and some in each year except 1949. The last eighty-seven engines (118) were lighter than the MZA and earlier RENFE ones, about 15·65 tons less.

These post-1940 Spanish 4–8–0s were delivered in successive years, starting in 1942, to the number of 31, 39, 5, 15, 23, 11, 9, nil, 32, 22, 51, and 4; the different builders' totals were B & W 52, Devis (later Macosa) 54, MTM 55, and Euskalduna 81. These numbers do not include the delivery of fifteen Andaluces 4200s from Devis in 1942, nor eight Oeste 1000s, also from Devis, in 1940. The total was 242.

All but one of these RENFE 4–8–0 engines were still at work in 1969, but, except for seventy-five MZA ones of class 1400, all the companies' classes had been withdrawn.

Six 4–8–0s (82) were built in Spain for export to Portugal and except for details were duplicates of Oeste class 1000 (109). That the Spanish locomotive

building industry was able to build them when every effort was being made to provide for Spain's own needs, indicates that relations between the countries were very cordial.

A comparison of the dimensions of Spanish 4–8–0s built over the period 1912 to 1953, or from 1918 for the home-built engines, indicates what progress was made. This is the more remarkable as the earliest of them were quite advanced designs.

The total number of 4–8–0s built for Spanish railways was 802, more than for any other country, but the Hungarian State Railways hold the record for the largest number of 4–8–0s of one class, with the PLM of France second and the RENFE third. Undoubtedly the 4–8–0 is to be regarded as a classic Iberian locomotive type.

Conclusion

The 4–8–0 type was built for the railways of Europe for over half a century and has worked there for over two-thirds of a century and may do so for several years yet. The total number built in and for Europe may be estimated at about 2,000. That it lasted so long shows that it was well suited to railway conditions, mainly in hilly and mountainous countries.

In the hands of a master locomotive designer it was the type chosen for one of the most, if not the most, outstanding steam locomotive classes ever built, in Europe or anywhere else.

CHAPTER 3

AFRICA

SECTION 9

(a) Related though Separated

THE railways of Africa differ from those of either Europe or North America. The railways of North America form a vast network of lines, on which vehicles move with little restriction, and those of Europe permit a large measure of inter-running; those of Africa form no system for the whole continent and some individual territories have several unconnected lines, sometimes of different gauges. The locomotives do tend to have common features, partly because so many were for the numerous British dependencies or for railways elsewhere, built by British interests.

Most railways in Africa are narrow gauge, the 3ft 6in and metre gauges predominating.

For the 4–8–0 type those built for the Cape Government Railways in 1892 were the first of that wheel arrangement in Africa and were the design from which almost all others were derived. From South Africa the 4–8–0 spread to Bechuanaland and Rhodesia, to Angola and Mozambique, to the Belgian Congo, to Nigeria and the Gold Coast, to Nyasaland, to German East Africa, to Kenya and Uganda, to Sierra Leone, and to the Sudan and/or Egypt; often it was not just the 4–8–0 but the CGR's first variety of 4–8–0 that spread in this way. This 'Cape' design had an influence on many 3ft 6in and metre gauge 4–8–0s built in Great Britain for railways far from Africa and for many years.

What was this ancestral engine like and what sort of railway did it run over? Most African railways run inland from the coast and are faced with a climb over the mountainous rim of an inland plateau; most had to be built cheaply so light track, steep grades, and sharp curves were normal. These conditions demanded light, powerful locomotives with low axle loads, but good adhesive weight. There was no question of anything but low or moderate speeds.

(b) The 7th Class

The first African 4–8–0 tender engines were the 7th class of the Cape Government Railways (119) and what immediately strikes anyone used to later South African locomotives is the squat look due to the low pitch of the boiler, the long chimney, high dome and upstanding cab (Fig 42). The coupled wheels were small, and the leading pair had flangeless tyres. They were small with a maximum axle load of 9 tons, just over 35 tons adhesive and $45\frac{1}{2}$ tons total engine weight. They were built by Dübs & Co and by Neilson & Co, both of Glasgow, six from the former, works Nos 2882-7, runnings Nos 315-20, and thirty-two from the latter, works Nos 4446-77 and running Nos 321-52. The Neilson engines were all alike, but half their tenders were six-wheeled and half with bogies. The design was due to the chief locomotive superintendent, M. Stephens, with Gregory & Eyles as consulting engineers. Special grates were provided to suit the South African coal. They ran steadily at 30mph and hauled 206 tons up 7 miles of 1 in 40 with 7 chain curves at a mean speed of $6\frac{1}{2}$mph, a fair performance remembering they were saturated steam engines with low boiler pressure and that train resistance was higher then than it is now.

The CGR 7th class continued to be built with modifications until 1913: the South African Railways eventually owned seven varieties of the class in all. After the 38 class 7 engines built in 1892 came 27 class 7A (120) in 1896, 3 in 1897, 13 in 1898 and 1 in 1901, making 44, then 28 class 7B (121) in 1900, 10 7C (122) in 1902, and so on to 5 7D (123), 7 7E (124) and 3 7F (125). Class 7A came from Sharp, Stewart & Co as well as Dübs and Neilson, 14, 21, and 9 locomotives, respectively; all the rest

54

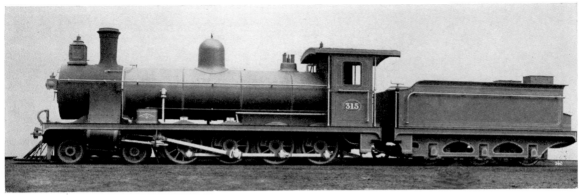

Fig 42 *Cape Government Railways 7th class of 1892, with six-wheeled tender*

from Neilson (or Neilson, Reid) except the last 5, which were from North British after the amalgamation. Elsewhere a near derivative of this class was built as late as 1930. The 7th class reached Bechuanaland in 1896 or 1897, when some were hired from the CGR for the line from Vryburg to Bulawayo. In 1897 four of the 7th class were built by Neilson for the Bechuanaland Railway (126), which was worked by the CGR until at least 1903, though some locomotives may have belonged to Rhodesia Railways. Some, probably six, of the Cape engines were taken over by RR later in 1897 and ten new ones were built for them in 1900 by Neilson, Reid & Co as the firm had become in 1897 (127); these had Belpaire fireboxes.

The next appearance of the 7th class was at the opposite end of Africa when the Egyptian War Office ordered three from Neilson who shipped them in 1897 for the *Soudan Military Railway* (128). Two and then three more followed soon. They incorporated special features: provision was made for coupling a water tank in front and for working without the tender, there being railings across the back of the cab.

The last stretch of railway up the Nile valley in Egypt was then being built to 3ft 6in gauge, but was far from finished. Another 3ft 6in gauge line was under construction in the Sudan up the Nile valley from Wadi Halfa. As both were 'military railways' it is not clear if the 4–8–0s worked north or south of the frontier or both. The Suakin & Berber was a military railway in the Sudan, but was usually referred to by name. Some 4–8–0s eventually passed to the Sudan Government Railways and worked there for many years.

When the 7th class penetrated from Cape Colony into the Orange Free State and the Transvaal the author has not found out, but the ZASM, the Central South African Railway Company, certainly had some, built for the CGR between 1892 and 1898 and some built in 1900 by Neilson on an order for twenty-five from the British War Office for the CGR, Nos 106-30, Neilson's Nos 5813-37. In 1901 Neilson built three for the Pretoria & Pietersburg Railway, which became ZASM Nos 398-400. There was exchange of locomotives with Rhodesian Railways as their No 1 of 1900 became ZASM No 380 and Neilson's No 5814 became Beira & Mashonaland Railway No 19. It is probable that all twenty-five, except No 5814 and three others that reached the Natal Government Railways, passed to the ZASM, as twenty-five engines from that railway were later classed as 7B by the SAR, together with the three from Natal. Some ZASM 7th class engines were rebuilt by 1905 with larger boilers (129) (Fig 43).

The Mashonaland and Beira railways were at first separate undertakings and physically separate from the Rhodesia Railway; initial construction was on 2ft 0in gauge working inland from the, sometimes, navigable Pungwe river in Mozambique. The line was soon widened to 3ft 6in gauge and virtually rebuilt and extended to Beira. The climb from the coast involved long 1 in 50 gradients and frequent 5 chain curves. The line was lightly constructed so the choice of the Cape 7th class is no surprise; in the first years of the twentieth century they entered service there (130) introducing the 4–8–0 to Mozambique.

In 1900 Neilson built Cape 7th class engines for the B & MR and in 1901 a dozen for the Rhodesia

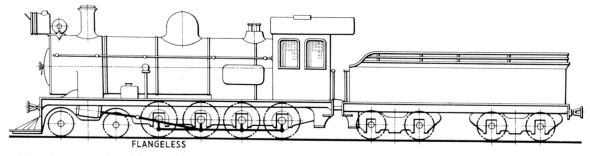

FLANGELESS

Fig 43 A re-boiled Central South African Railway 7th class locomotive; the patch on the firebox side is a cover giving access to the Drummond transverse water-tubes

Railway, works Nos 5791-802, but 5791-2 became B & M Nos 21-2 and 5797 No 23. At some later date five class 7 engines from the B & MR, dating from 1900, passed to the SAR as class 7D.

The Benguela Railway in Angola acquired four 7th class locomotives in 1907 and 1908 from the Avonside Engine Company, of Bristol. As Robert Williams, the moving spirit of the Benguela, was a personal friend of Cecil Rhodes, with his well-known interest in development of African railways, the choice was natural; these engines were afterwards modified, for they became wood burners (131), of which more later.

This was not the end of the construction of these Cape engines for by 1909 both the Lagos Railway and the Baro–Kano Railway, in the south and north of Nigeria respectively, had 'modified' 7th class engines in service and the Gold Coast Railway had some a little smaller built in that year.

The Bas Congo Katanga Railway in the Belgian Congo obtained some engines of the same design in 1911, built in 1909 by the Société St Léonard of Liège. Lastly in 1912 the 7th class reached Nyasaland in modified form, these too being a little smaller.

For a single design of locomotive to have been so widespread and to have been built for such a long time implies that it was well suited to African conditions and very soundly conceived in the first place.

Having followed the 7th class round the continent it will now be easier to follow the development of the 4–8–0 country by country.

The 4–8–0 made its appearance in Cape Colony in 1892; in Rhodesia, Bechuanaland, and the Sudan or Egypt by 1897; in the Transvaal, OFS, and Mozambique by 1901; in Natal by 1904; in Angola in 1908; in the Gold Coast and Nigeria in 1909; in the Belgian Congo by 1911; in Sierra Leone in 1911;

Fig 44 The New Cape Central Railway's 1913 7th class, later South African Railways class 7F

in Nyasaland and German East Africa by 1912; and in Kenya in 1914.

(c) South Africa

In Cape Colony besides fifty-seven more 7th class engines that had been built, with modifications, from 1896 to 1902 by Dübs, Sharp Stewart, and Neilson for the Cape Government Railways, twenty-five were ordered by the British War Office, most of which were diverted to the ZASM. The New Cape Central Railway, which worked a line owned by the Cape Government, had a succession of 7th class engines, four built by Neilson in 1899 and 1900 and two in 1903, ordered from Neilson, but delivered by North British, one in 1904 and three in 1913 (Fig 44) from North British: these became SAR class 7E and 7F.

More powerful engines being required in 1901, three 8th class 4–8–0s were ordered from Neilson and built in 1902, followed by further batches of ten, ten, twelve, and six in that year, the last with the boiler centre raised 1in, and six in 1903 (132).

Meanwhile in the Transvaal and the Orange Free State also larger locomotives were needed and 20 8th class were built in 1902 by Neilson (133); 20 more came in 1902 from Sharp Stewart (134), and then 60 ordered from Neilson, but 50 of them delivered by North British (135) and another 20 in 1903 from North British. At least ten of them had Drummond water-tubes in their fireboxes (136) (Fig 45). Some of the reboilered 7th class also had them; they were not satisfactory. The later 1902 and 1903 engines became classes 8A and 8B of the SAR. All these were designed by H. Beatty, chief locomotive superintendent of the CGR, with Gregory & Eyles and Sir Douglas Fox and Sir Charles Metcalfe, Bart, as consulting engineers. They had bar frames with the firebox above them, but between the wheels. Later in 1903, a further modification was the use of a wider firebox and grate with the foundation ring above the fourth and arched over the third pair of coupled wheels, then tapered inwards just to go between the second pair. The grate area was thus increased by 29 per cent with some benefit to the performance of these four engines (137) (Fig 46), later class 8E. The abnormal shape of the foundation ring may have led to heavy maintenance. Ten class 8F followed in 1903/4 (138).

By 1904 there were seven varieties of the 8th class on the railways that formed the SAR. Both the 7th and 8th classes were subsequently given new boilers with superheaters. Of the former at least twenty-five were so treated (139) with no change in dimensions of cylinders or boiler pressure; of the latter all varieties were involved in two different conversions. In one, new cylinders of 19in diameter were fitted and in the other 20in cylinders, both with piston valves. The new boilers were the same for all. Those with larger cylinders had their wheelbase increased between the bogie and leading coupled wheels (140) and (141).

The CGR had one other 4–8–0 classified as 'Experimental No 6' or 10th class, built by Kitson in 1906. It was larger than the 8th class (142). Although the first reports were favourable it was not repeated; preference was given to types with a trailing truck.

The 4–8–0 tender engine was used in Natal and might have been used earlier had not the Natal Government Railways had a predilection for tank engines, which they developed up to the well-known

Fig 45 *A Central South African Railway 8th class with Drummond transverse water-tubes in the firebox*

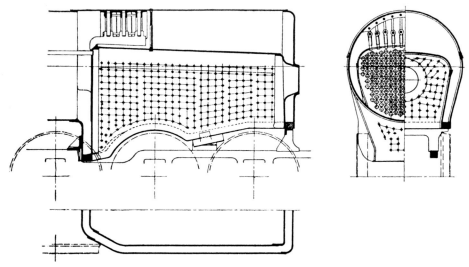

Fig 46 *The firebox of South African Railways class 8E showing the specially shaped foundation ring*

4-10-2T type. Eventually the NGR made use of tender engines, many being designed by D. Hendrie, and North British built fifty 'Hendrie B' 4-8-0s in 1904 (143) (Fig 47). The NGR a few years later fitted a trailing truck carrying only 2½ tons to the last six of them making them 4-8-2s. The object was to obtain smoother running when working passenger trains. Before being converted back to 4-8-0s they were claimed to be the first 4-8-2 tender engines in the world. In August 1909 twenty-one 'Improved Hendrie B' locomotives were ordered from North British (144) and eighteen were in service by May 1910. The Natal 4-8-0s became SAR classes 1 and 1A. The last of the 1As had piston instead of slide valves.

In 1910 the South African Railways came into being at the same time as the Union of South Africa. The last Natal 4-8-0s were thus delivered to the SAR. The NGR had three of the Cape 7th class, but when they reached Natal or passed to the NGR the author cannot say.

Two other classes of 4-8-0 just come within the purview of this work and hailed from the ZASM, namely SAR classes 13 and 17. Thirty of the former were built as 4-10-2T tank engines and rebuilt as 4-8-0 tender engines retaining their side tanks (145) (Fig 48). On the ZASM they were class E built in 1901 for the Imperial Military Force. They had small six-wheeled tenders from obsolete engines. The 17th class (146) dated from 1890 to 1900 and were built

Fig 47 *A Natal Government Railways 'Hendrie B', later* SAR *class 1*

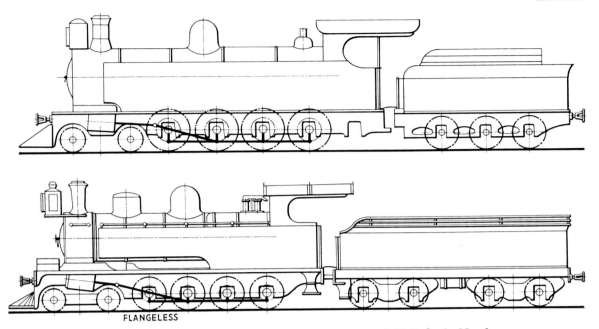

FLANGELESS

Fig 48 *South African Railways classes 13 (above) and 17 (below); Natal type tank engines rebuilt with tenders*

as 4–8–2Ts by Dübs for Natal; twenty–one were converted (Fig 48).

In 1946 the SAR had 348 4–8–0s in service and some 7th class were in use in 1969. The number built for the predecessors of the SAR is doubtful due to the exchanges, hiring, and taking over of unrecorded numbers, but was about 380 from North British and its predecessors, mostly from Neilson. A number have been sold to various colliery and other industrial railways and some were fitted with Giesl 'ejectors' in 1970. The 380 do not include the fifty-one conversions.

SECTION 10

(a) Central Africa

In Rhodesia some 7th class, of which fifty-one were built from 1897 to 1906, by Neilson, North British, and Kitson, besides those transferred from the CGR, were in service until the early 1960s, including some that were rebuilt as tank engines. One of this class is preserved and still occasionally hauls historic special trains on suitable occasions. Some of the eight engines (147) built by Kitson in 1901 were commandeered by the British War Office and diverted to the CGR, but eventually reached Rhodesia.

Several 7th class engines were sold by Rhodesia Railways, seven to the Zambesi Sawmills Company's railway, three to the Congo, three to the Mozambique Railways, and one to the SAR besides the earlier transfer of five already mentioned.

The RR's 8th class (148) were Beatty engines with minor modifications and ten were built in 1904. The second and third batches (149) of 1910 and 1911, totalling seven, differed in the firebox and were heavier, all from North British. Four were sold to Zambesi Sawmills. North British built eighteen RR 9th class 4–8–0s in 1911-12. In 1915 Beyer, Peacock & Co Ltd of Gorton, Manchester, built six 9th class (150) (Fig 49) and North British six more in 1916; by 1917 thirty were in service.

The author recalls that when he was at Gorton Foundry he helped, in 1928 or 1929, to forge a foundation ring for a replacement boiler for one of these 4–8–0s. The 9th class were superheated from the start.

Fig 49 *A Rhodesia Railways class 9, of 1915*

Due to the delay in delivery from Great Britain during the first world war, six 4–8–0s were ordered in 1915 from the Montreal Locomotive Works; they were an Americanised 9th class, classified 9A (151). During and after the second world war twenty-five 9th class were fitted with larger boilers and became class 9B (152).

The increase in size of the 4–8–0 in Rhodesia from 7th to 9th class and to 9B is typical of the change on African railways between 1897 and 1911 and of the effects of war. There is the same raising of the boiler as in America and Europe, affected by the African engines being of narrow gauge.

The first 4–8–0s to work in Mozambique were those of the Mashonaland Railway, which operated the Beira and the Beira Junction railways; they were the ubiquitous 7th class and are included in those of Rhodesia Railways. Later the Canadian class 9A en-gines worked mainly in Mozambique until displaced by Garratts.

Some of the railways built to serve Nyasaland lay partly or wholly in Mozambique. First the Shiré Highlands Railway in Nyasaland connected the Shiré river to Blantyre and later to Lake Nyasa; then the Central Africa Railway connected the Shiré Highlands Railway to the Zambesi and was partly in Nyasaland and partly in Mozambique; the line was built because the lower part of the Shiré could only sometimes be navigated. The Zambesi itself was not always navigable and so the Trans-Zambesia Railway was built to connect the railway near Beira to the Zambesi with a ferry for crossing the river. The great Lower Zambesi bridge was still in the future.

The Central Africa and Shiré Highlands railways were operated as one, later being fused as Nyasaland

Fig 50 *A 1912 wood burner for the Shiré Highlands Railway*

Fig 51 *A Nyasaland Railways 4–8–0 of 1930, fitted with a feed-water heater*

Railways. These lines had similar 4–8–0s that were virtually 7th class, but wood burning and with smaller coupled wheels. The Hunslet Engine Company Ltd, of Leeds, built one for the Shiré Highlands in 1912 (153) (Fig 50) and some for the Central Africa came from R. & W. Hawthorn, Leslie & Co, of Newcastle upon Tyne, in 1915 (154). Two similar engines were built by Hawthorn Leslie in 1921 (155) for the Trans-Zambesia Railway. The Lower Zambesi bridge and its approach railways finally completed the chain of railways from Beira to Lake Nyasa some dozen years later. Six more 4–8–0s were ordered from North British by the Central Africa in 1930 (156) (Fig 51). Nyasaland Railways had thirteen 4–8–0s in service in 1958.

The northward extension of the Rhodesia Railways reached the frontier of the Belgian Congo in November 1909. The Katanga Railway continued through Elizabethville to Bukama, whence the Bas Congo Katanga Railway ran northwestwards towards the lower Congo, now terminating at Port Franqui, with river transport beyond. A branch connects to the Benguela Railway.

The Katanga copper belt produces traffic for these railways. In 1909 the Société Anonyme de St Léonard of Liège, Belgium, built five 4–8–0s for the BCK (157). A French commentator on the one shown at the Brussels exhibition remarked on its 'English' appearance: it was a Cape 7th class engine in almost all details! Six more followed in 1911, built by the Société Anonyme des Forges, Usines et Fonderies, Haine St Pierre (Fig 52); they were about a ton heavier and the boiler pressure was 171lb/sq in. These were for the Katanga Railway.

Fig 52 *A Katanga Railway '7th class' of 1912; like those for Rhodesia built in 1903 they had Belpaire fireboxes*

Fig 53 *The Benguela Railway's wood-burning 8th class were more like the Cape 'Experimental 6' than the Cape 8th class*

The Benguela Railway, CFB, runs across Angola from east to west and was built to provide a second railway to the Katanga copper belt. Being British financed, it obtained most of its locomotives from Great Britain and sampled the products of at least seven British builders. There was a good proportion of 4–8–0s and they were of the 7th (131), 8th (158) and the 9th classes (159) similar to the Cape and to the Rhodesian classes of these designations, but they were or became wood burners. This railway owns vast areas of timber plantations along its line and grows much of its fuel to this day, but now has a few oil-burning locomotives at the coastal end of the line, where the earliest engines burned coal.

Kitson built two 8th class locomotives for this line in 1910 (Fig 53). Two 9th class were built in 1914 by North British, but due to the first world war, a couple were ordered from Baldwin and sup-

plied in 1920 (160). North British built ten, with larger tenders, in 1924 and eighteen (161) (Fig 54) in 1929. There were thirty-eight 4–8–0s on the Benguela in all.

North of the Benguela another line traverses Angola in a mainly west-to-east direction; this is the Luanda, or Loanda, Railway. It was originally of metre gauge, but was converted to 3ft 6in some years ago. For this line a dozen 4–8–0s were ordered from Sir W. G. Armstrong, Whitworth & Co Ltd of Newcastle upon Tyne in March 1923 (162) (Fig 55): Henschel supplied nine (163) (Fig 55) in the same year, these being smaller. Beyer, Peacock prepared a 4–8–0 design for this railway in January 1923, but seem to have been underbidden.

To the south of the Benguela the Moçamedes (or Mossâmedes) Railway runs inland from the coast and was partly converted relatively recently from

Fig 54 *A Benguela Railway 9th class of 1929*

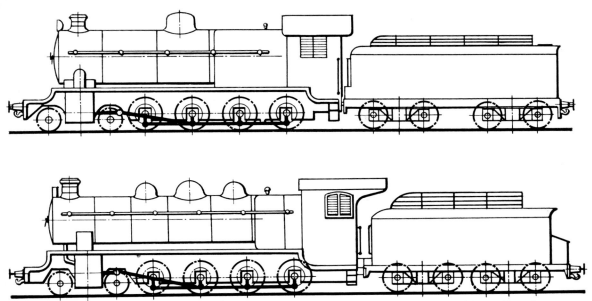

Fig 55 *The Luanda Railway's class 200 (above) built by Armstrong, Whitworth and class 150 (below) by Henschel, both in 1923*

narrow to 3ft 6in gauge. This line too had some 4–8–0s, four built by Avonside (164) and two by Kitson (165), obtained secondhand from the Benguela in 1955; also one Henschel and two Armstrong Whitworth 4–8–0s like those for the Luanda.

(b) West Africa

Both the Gold Coast and Nigeria had their first 4–8–0s in 1909. In Nigeria the Lagos Railway had four 'Modified Cape 7th Class' engines and the Baro–Kano Railway had five 'Modified CSAR Class 7' ones, but the CSAR (ZASM) locomotives differed little from the Cape ones. They were built in 1908 and went into service next year. One modification as compared with the Cape engines was a Belpaire instead of a round-topped firebox (166). Two followed, one each in 1910 and 1911: North British were the builders. They formed the '244-254' class of the Nigerian Railway, an amalgamation of the earlier railways. Two were rebuilt, superheated, about 1934 (167) when the rest were withdrawn; the rebuilt ones ran till 1951. The Lagos Railway ordered two 4–8–0s in 1911, from Nasmyth, Wilson & Co Ltd, the first superheated locomotives (168) in Nigeria; these also were rebuilt in 1934 (169) and ran until 1950.

The next 4–8–0s were ordered by the Nigerian Railway and built in batches from 1912 to 1923; they totalled forty-four (170) (Fig 56). For seven years they worked the traffic north of Jebba, where 45lb/yd rails were laid. They were Nos 257-300; the first three came from Nasmyth, Wilson in 1912 and two more in 1914, running Nos 257-61 and works Nos 966-8 and 1024-5. Meanwhile, North British had built Nos 262-8 in 1914 in two batches, a special premium being offered for delivery of the second lot before May: Nos 269-81 were ordered from NB Locomotive in August 1914 and built in 1915. The rest were post-war, nineteen being built by William Beardsmore & Co of Dalmuir, Glasgow.

Between 1913 and 1922 another variety of 4–8–0 was built for the Nigerian Railway, totalling thirty-two engines (171) (Fig 57); they were Nos 301-32, the first four from North British were appreciably larger than the previous engines. A dozen, Nos 305-16, followed from NB in 1915. The rest were ordered in 1919 and these sixteen were built by Armstrong Whitworth. In 1927 eight were rebuilt into 4–8–2 engines, with much larger boilers. Eight more were rebuilt between 1935 and 1942 with larger boilers, but still as 4–8–0s (172) and five had new cylinders. The rebuilds could haul 50 to 100 tons more, steamed better, and used less fuel and water.

Fig 56 *One of the '257-300' class of the Nigerian Railway; the general appearance is very like that of the earlier '244-254' class, originally built for the Lagos and Baro-Kano railways*

Fig 57 *One of the Nigerian Railway's larger '301-332' class*

Fig 58 *A more modern Nigerian 4–8–0 of the '601-605' class*

Fig 59 *A Gold Coast Government Railway's 4–8–0 of 1911*

The class was withdrawn in 1946, but two engines were in service in 1951. At about the same time three unsuperheated 4–8–0s, Nos 151-3, were supplied by North British for construction work on the Nigerian Railway eastern line between Port Harcourt and Enugu late in 1914 and three in 1922 by Vulcan Foundry Ltd of Newton-le-Willows, Lancashire, Nos 154-6. These lasted until various years between 1936 and 1950 (173).

Five 4–8–0s, numbered 601-5, were built by Beyer Peacock in 1919 (174) (Fig 58) for the light rail section north of Jebba and six Nos 211-16, by Nasmyth, Wilson, in 1923 (175) for construction work north of Enugu.

The last 4–8–0s for the Nigerian Railway were twenty-eight in number (176). Three were built by Nasmyth, Wilson in 1924 and in 1925 North British built three lots of four, twelve, and three. Six were built by Robert Stephenson & Co, of Darlington, in 1928. They were numbered 606-33.

Except for superheating and improved design and construction of boilers, cylinders and valve gear, the later engines were little changed from the originals, but their performance had much improved. The rebuilding and re-boilering had the same effect in bettering performance, larger boilers provided more steam and better valve gear let it be used more effectively and loads were increased. In one conversion the engines received larger coupled wheels and could make better time with the same load.

On the Gold Coast Railways the 4–8–0s of 1909 were smaller than Nigeria's and had smaller coupled wheels, but were much like the 7th class. Nine engines (177) built by Hawthorn, Leslie lasted in service until between 1934 and 1938, working mainly on the Sekondi–Kumasi line. In 1911 two more (Fig 59) came from Hunslet, entering service in 1912.

Hawthorn, Leslie built four superheated 4–8–0s (178) in 1914. Six were ordered from Hawthorns in 1918, but delivery was not made until 1920, in which year seven were ordered from North British. They were under-boilered: the cylinders of one were lined up from 18 to 17in diameter with beneficial results, but not enough to warrant treating the rest likewise. Some of them were running on the Prestea branch in 1952.

The Sierra Leone Government Railway has a gauge of 2ft 6in and a maximum permitted axle load of 5 tons. It is the oldest railway in any of the former British West African territories. The line follows the lie of the land as far as possible so that 1 in 50 grades and curves abound, with one much steeper bank in Freetown itself. The first 4–8–0s for this line were built by Nasmyth Wilson in 1910 and were small even for 2ft 6in gauge (179) (Fig 60); they must have been serviceable as four more came from Nasmyth, Wilson in 1913. Six built by Hawthorn, Leslie, entered service in 1914-15 and five, this time from North British, in 1922. In 1944 twenty 4–8–0s entered service, half built by Andrew Barclay, Sons & Co Ltd, of Kilmarnock, and half by W. G. Bagnall Ltd, of Stafford (180). Twenty-four 4–8–0s were running in the late 1940s. The weight of the last batch of engines was 2·625 tons more than the first, an increase of 13 per cent. The last lot had bogie, instead of six-wheeled, tenders. The design prepared by Beyer, Peacock in August 1909

E

Fig 60 *A Sierra Leone Government Railway's 4–8–0 of 1910 some thirty years later.*
Compare Fig 87

had a bogie tender; perhaps that made it more costly so their offer was not accepted. The 1913 lot had Drummond steam driers.

These engines were not derived from the Cape locomotives, or influenced by them beyond the fact that the widespread use of the 7th class had shown that the 4–8–0 wheel arrangement was suitable for a variety of African conditions.

(c) East Africa

In German East Africa there were two railways of metre gauge, the Usambara Railway near the Kenya frontier and the Tanganyika Railway, which crossed the middle of the territory roughly east to west.

The Tanganyika line was begun at Dar es Salaam in 1905, reached Morogoro in two years and was being extended to Tabora. It was opened through to Lake Tanganyika in February 1914, but was hardly finished before the outbreak of war, in East Africa as in Europe, affected the line and led to much destruction of bridges and rolling stock.

The railway had been supplied with some 4–8–0s of German design and construction (181), some having been built by Borsig in 1912. Despite efforts to destroy locomotives and rolling stock by blowing up bridges and running trains into the gaps, the Royal Engineers got some 4–8–0s going again, as those near the tops of the piles of wreckage were little damaged.

During hostilities in East Africa locomotives were sent from India, including some 4–8–0s, besides some built in 1916 by Nasmyth, Wilson for the Nizam's State Railway, that were commandeered and delivered direct to Africa. Whether they remained in what became Tanganyika Territory or reached or returned to India, the author has not discovered; their description will be left to Section 15 (b).

The first British-built locomotives intended for Tanganyika Railways were built by Beyer, Peacock in 1923. They were six in number and were a wood-burning version (182) (Fig 61) of a Uganda Railway class. In 1926 six were ordered from Vulcan Foundry, builders of similar engines for the Uganda

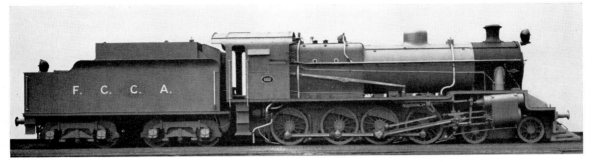

Fig 65 *One of the last 4–8–0s built by North British, the Central Argentine's later oil burners*

in and oil burners. Few people then thought that during a second world war, as during the first, Argentine locomotives, including these 4–8–0s, would have to use maize as fuel. Trials were carried out with No 778, one of the simples, and the outcome was the use of a mixture of coal and maize, 60/40 for fast goods, 50/50 for through goods, and 40/60 for pick-up goods. The calorific value of maize is about a third that of Welsh steam coal, but in Argentina the price too was about a third and in 1942 coal was very scarce. During the depression years locomotives in Brazil used unsaleable coffee as fuel. The steam locomotive *could* function, if not to the full, on such unusual and inferior fuels when necessity arose.

In 1945 a further twenty simples were ordered from North British and in 1948 Robert Stephenson & Hawthorn supplied five 4–8–0s, these being a modernised version of the two-cylinder simple, with boiler pressure raised to 225lb/sq in (193) (Fig 65);

they were oil burners like the earlier compounds.

The Buenos Ayres Great Southern Railway acquired its first 4–8–0s, twenty-five in number, in 1924; classified 11C, they were three-cylinder simples and were built by Armstrong, Whitworth. One of them (194) was shown that year at the British Empire exhibition at Wembley. They had three separate sets of valve gear and all three sets of motion drove the second coupled axle. They were larger than the earlier Central Argentine 4–8–0s. They were shipped fully erected from Newcastle, a procedure then sufficiently novel for comment in the press, at least when so large a consignment was involved. A further fifty were built in 1928, thirty by Armstrong, Whitworth and twenty by Beyer, Peacock (195) (Fig 66) with larger tenders. The author remembers that these tenders were sent by road from Gorton to either Liverpool or Birkenhead for shipment; one came to grief on the way under an arch bridge as the lorry driver failed to go under

Fig 66 *Class 11C of the Buenos Ayres Great Southern Railway; one of the second batch*

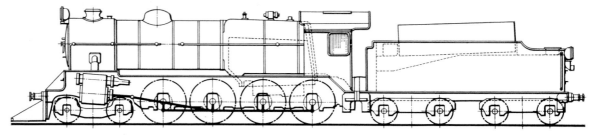

Fig 67 *Class 15B of the Buenos Ayres Great Southern Railway; one of the last 4–8–0s built by Vulcan Foundry*

the centre of the arch. The tender was soon repaired, but the bridge carried the scars for many years and perhaps still does so. Four of them were later converted to burn coal, the tenders being adapted accordingly.

The BAGS received eight two-cylinder 4–8–0s in 1938 from Vulcan Foundry (196). The boiler pressure had gone up to 225lb/sq in and the tenders were still larger; the driving wheels were larger than for the earlier class 11C engines as the later ones were for fast freight and perishable goods trains. Eleven years later thirty came from Vulcan (197) (Fig 67), the weight reduced some tons by improved design and construction. These two series were FCS classes 15A and 15B. The seventy-five BAGS class 11C 4–8–0s were modified by the FC General Roca in 1958-9 to the designs of André Chapelon, by then retired from active service with the SNCF. The list of modifications is long, but the cost of the work was moderate, about a seventh of that of a general overhaul. The boiler pressure was raised as much as the boiler design permitted; alterations to the small tubes reduced the proportion of gasses passing through the flues; lengthening the superheater elements was permitted by use of an improved burner enabling combustion to end in the firebox with no post-combustion in the flues; new combination levers for the valve gear; new liners for the valve chests; new kinds of ring for valves and pistons; improved exhaust passages and a single Kylchap exhaust instead of the plain rectangular blast-pipe cap. As the object was to obtain greater power as well as greater economy, frame strengthening was undertaken, especially the cross bracing; automatically adjusted wedges were fitted to the driving axle horns and mechanical lubricators fitted for bearings, valves, and pistons, besides some minor improvements. The re-built engines (197) gave a power increase, for the same fuel consumption, of from 26 to 40 per

cent, depending on the speed and power output; for the same power they needed 16 to 40 per cent less fuel. These figures were the outcome of careful comparative tests.

After the modifications the average fuel consumption hauling freight trains of 1,500 to 2,000 tons, was about 30 per cent lower than before and so much had the performance improved that they took over duties from larger and more recently built 4–8–0s, such as haulage of fast perishable traffic, despite their smaller wheels.

The Buenos Aires Central was one of the few standard-gauge railways in Argentina and was Argentine financed and operated, being one of the Lacroze family interests. For this line Kerr Stuart & Company, Ltd, of Stoke-on-Trent, built six 4–8–0s (199) (Fig 68) in 1929, to the requirements of Señor Oscar Jaette; they were coal burners of a simple and straightforward design. Beyer, Peacock prepared a 4–8–0 design in the autumn of 1931, but nothing came of it due to the onset of the economic slump.

The Buenos Ayres Western Railway was later in receiving its 4–8–0s in 1931. As originally planned they would have had cast steel bar frames, cast steel cylinders, and 225lb/sq in boiler pressure, but the builders, Armstrong, Whitworth, could not provide the steel castings and the engines were redesigned with plate frames and cast-iron cylinders, with consequent weight increase. To compensate, the boiler was made lighter by using thinner plates, pressure reduced to 200lb/sq in and the cylinder bore increased from $19\frac{1}{2}$ to $20\frac{1}{2}$in (200). It is of interest that Beyer, Peacock prepared a plate-framed 4–8–0 design for the FCO in February, 1930, with cylinders 20in bore × 28in stroke, driving 5ft 8in diameter coupled wheels. At first these engines had side play in the bearings of the trailing coupled axles, but later this was taken up and thin flanges provided on the wheels of the driving and intermediate axles.

Fig 68 *Six engines for the Buenos Aires Central Railway awaiting shipment at Birkenhead; the tenders have already been loaded*

The Argentine Great Western Railway may have had a class of 4–8–0s, but the author has not fully established their existence. When the GOA acquired some Garratts in 1930 the trains they hauled were stated to be 85 per cent heavier than those hauled by 4–8–0s (201). The author has found no trace of such engines being built either for the GOA or for the BAP, with which it was affiliated. They might have been secondhand.

Reverting to the Argentine State Railways, in

the latter part of the 1940s, the Argentine engineer, L. D. Porta, undertook the rebuilding of a 4–6–2 as a four-cylinder compound 4–8–0, inspired by the Chapelon rebuilt engines described in Section 7 (b); on a smaller scale this was similarly successful. The boiler pressure was 285lb/sq in, which meant a new welded boiler built without using press blocks; an intermediate superheater was fitted between the high- and low-pressure cylinders. In the period 1947 to 1949 the condition of the track did not permit

Fig 69 La Argentina, *L. D. Porta's 'Rebuilt Pacific' for the General Belgrano Railway. (Reproduced by permission of the Council of the Institution of Mechanical Engineers)*

the locomotive to attain its top design speed of 75 mph, but it did haul trains of 1,200 tons at up to 65mph and freight trains of 2,000 tons at 50mph; the riding of the engine was quite good at 65mph despite 4ft 1¼in coupled wheels. The maximum power output was 2,120hp at the drawbar, almost in proportion with that of the PO 4–8–0s in relation to the engine weights without tender, 69 to 109 tonnes. The locomotive was very efficient and economical in fuel consumption. It is unfortunate that money was not forthcoming for more such locomotives (202) (Fig 69) to be built, for the prototype was an outstanding engine.

SECTION 12

(a) Brazil and Peru

Brazil is the largest country in South America and its railways have only recently attained the state of a nearly connected system, but for a long time there have been quite large systems based on Rio de Janeiro and São Paulo. The Rio system includes the Central of Brazil, formerly the Dom Pedro Segundo Railway. As the Central main line makes its way inland it faces the ascent of the Serra do Mar, with long 1 in 55·5 grades and sharp curves; one bank averages 1 in 58 for 12½ miles. It is of 5ft 3in gauge.

In 1896 Brooks supplied some large 4–8–0s for this line. They were typically North American engines, that might have belonged to a railroad in the United States. The Brazilian ones were almost as large as the, then, most recent US 4–8–0s and some

later US ones were not so heavy. These Brazilian engines (203) (Fig 70) were quite advanced in design and may be compared with locomotives (14) to (28) in Table II. There may have been more from Alco later.

Further inland many lines of the Central Railway were of metre gauge, though some have since been converted to 1·6 metres. Some of the metre-gauge lines had heavy traffic and for them, too, Brooks built some 4–8–0s (204), which were sizeable for narrow gauge, being considerably larger than the US 3ft-gauge 4–8–0s of 1891 (13) in Table II, and nearly as large as the 3ft 6in-gauge Cape ones of 1892 (119) in Table IX. The author's information does not cover the number in either batch, or which were built first.

The Great Western of Brazil Railway was oddly named for, although the lines of which it was composed did run in a roughly westerly direction from the coast, they were in the most easterly part of the country. In 1905 North British built five metre-gauge 4–8–0s (205) (Fig 71) for this railway; the tenders had an unusual '2–4–0' wheel arrangement. Two followed in 1910 and three, superheated, in 1913, all from North British. Ten superheated 4–8–0s (206) were in service in 1926; the earlier engines had been superheated in 1913. In 1929 Armstrong, Whitworth built some rather more powerful 4–8–0s (207) for the GWB, of which the author knows that there were four, as he helped in loading some Garratts for shipment to Argentina and the same ship, the *Belpamela*, carried these engines and tenders to Brazil. Six 4–8–0s were still in service in 1970.

Fig 70 *Brooks broad gauge 4–8–0 of 1896 for the Central of Brazil Railway.*
(*Reproduced by courtesy of* The Engineer)

Fig 71 *The Great Western of Brazil Railway's 1905 4–8–0s had an unusual wheel arrangement for the tender*

In 1925 Henschel supplied three metre-gauge wood-burning 4–8–0s (208) to the Brazilian North Western Railway. They were larger than those for the GWB and more modern in design.

The number of 4–8–0s that ran in Brazil was quite small, but well spread out in both place and time.

In about 1907 some 4–8–0s were supplied to the Peruvian Corporation, which operated the more important railways in the country; but it is not clear if they were for service on the Central Railway of Peru, FCC, or the Southern Railway of Peru, FCS, or both.

The 'new' engines were too heavy for the bridges, which were being renewed; the Southern had fewer bridges than the Central and only one in 107 miles from Mollendo to Arequipa, which suggests that the 'Mastodon' engines would have been used there first. The Southern certainly had some 4–8–0s of US origin: the builders were Baldwin and Rogers, which

raises a question because in 1905 Rogers became a part of the American Locomotive Company. Were genuine Rogers locomotives supplied in, or before, 1905? Or were Rogers works plates being used by Alco at a later date? The Southern had at least one 4–8–0 built in their Arequipa workshops with imported major components. Both the Baldwin and the Rogers engines were typically North American of the period and were standard-gauge two-cylinder compounds (209) (210). The Southern of Peru climbs to 14,666ft in some 220 miles, drops to about 13,000, up again to 14,150, and down to about 10,000ft. There is some 1 in 25, but it is not a large proportion of the whole and there are long lengths of relatively easy grades; there are curves with a radius of 328ft; for such a line the 4–8–0 was a suitable type.

The Central of Peru has steeper and more continuous gradients than the Southern. It is no ordinary railway, which averages 1 in 30·1 for 73 miles!

Fig 72 *A 3ft gauge 4–8–0 for the Northwestern Railway of Peru*

From 12ft above sea level the main line climbs to 15,693ft in the summit tunnel, to 15,806ft on a branch, and nearly 40ft higher on a mineral siding. The main climb is from Chosica, 2,821ft, to Ticlio, 15,610ft, some 117½km by rail, but less in a straight line, as the railway has thirteen reversing places and constant loops and curves to gain height in the narrow, twisting, and precipitous valley. The maximum gradient is 4½ per cent, 1 in 22.22, and there is a lot of it. For so steep a line the 2–8–0 was preferred with more of its weight on the coupled axles. But this railway did have a class of 4–8–0s (211), which were rebuilds of 4–8–2s that gave excessive trouble due to slipping. They were oil burners and had narrow fireboxes so it was possible to modify the boilers by shortening the barrels and moving the fireboxes forward between the wheels. Thus rebuilt they were nominally less powerful, but more practical operating units.

A third railway to use 4–8–0s was the North Western of Peru, a line of 3ft 0in gauge, which had four such locomotives (212) (Fig 72) built by North British in 1911, works Nos 19560-3. Another followed in 1923, and a sixth in 1925. The two later engines were built as oil burners. As might be expected they were smaller than those for the two standard-gauge lines. This railway ran parallel to the Central from Callao to Lima, then northwestwards to Ancon and Huacho, both on the coast, then back into the mountains to Sayan.

No other railway in Peru used 4–8–0s as far as the author is aware.

(b) Colombia

Like all countries on the Pacific coast of South America, Colombia is very mountainous; the northern end of the Andes is not as high as that immense range is further south, but it is split into three separate chains with two deep valleys between. There were originally a number of well-separated railways and at least three gauges were used, 3ft, metre, and 3ft 6in. This situation has only been put right in recent times. All lines are now of 3ft gauge and new construction has produced a unified system. In the early 1920s there were a number of government and company owned railways, the latter being taken over by the State as occasion arose.

In 1925 some 4–8–0s were built to the designs of P. C. Dewhurst, in charge of mechanical engineering for the government railways. There were two sizes for the 3ft and one for the metre gauge. All three classes had similar characteristics and had some features in common with that engineer's earlier ones

for the Jamaican Government Railways. (See Section 4.)

The obvious differences between the 4ft 8½in gauge and the narrow-gauge ones are that the latter have outside bar frames and are lower in build, as expected for engines that had to run on tracks which were then in poor condition. Steps were being taken to improve the track and were pursued energetically enough to have an effect between the building of one batch of 4–8–0s and the next for the same railway.

Political and/or financial considerations caused the engines to be ordered from England, Germany, and the US, at first, and later in Belgium and Czechoslovakia. Two builders were involved in England and two in Belgium.

Conditions varied on the various railways, of which there were twenty-two, the major ones nationalised, but even those only gradually came under unified management. The 'Standard' engines were one of the first signs of unification and the 4–8–0s were a major group amongst them.

The 4–8–0s had the drive on the third coupled axle, had controlled side play for the trailing coupled axle, and blind tyres on the wheels of the leading one.

The Pacific Railway, FC del Pacifico, was the largest of eight Government lines concerned in 1925. Its main line starts at Buenaventura and climbs to nearly 5,200ft in just under 80 miles with 33½ miles averaging 1 in 46. The maximum grade is 1 in 23½, 4.25 per cent, compensated for curvature, there being some curves of 170ft radius, 33.7°, and 184ft quite common.

The first eight of the smaller 3ft 0in-gauge engines were for this line, but the order was divided between Kitson (213) (works Nos 5391-2, the first two Kitson engines for 1925), Berlin (formerly L. Schwartzkopff) (214) and Baldwin (215). They were to run on 45lb/yd rails and the track was appreciably improved while the deliveries were taking place. Each of the builders imparted a characteristic appearance to their locomotives with American, British, or German details, but leaving the strong family resemblance plain to see (Fig 73).

The Kitson engines were the first and in the short time before the Berlin ones were built the latter could be heavier and have the boilers set higher, allowing better air access to the grate and better ashpans. The Berlin engines were tried with flanges on the leading coupled wheels and the intermediate pair blind, but they were soon altered to standard. A few years later engines of the larger 3ft 0in-gauge type were supplied to the Pacifico by Baldwin.

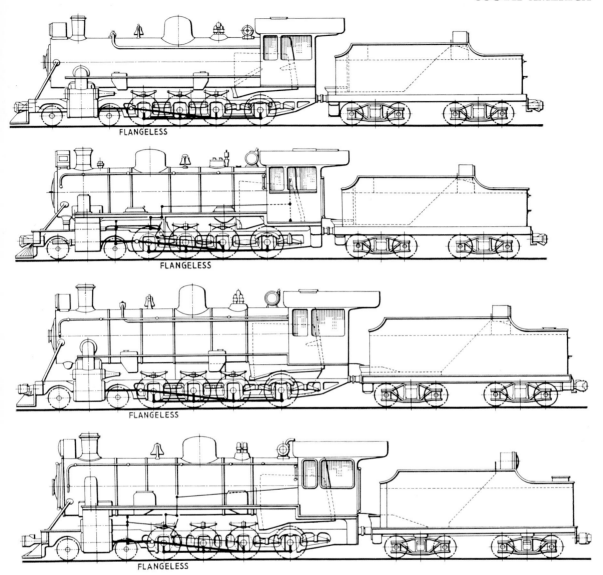

FLANGELESS

FLANGELESS

FLANGELESS

FLANGELESS

Fig 73 *The builders' national characteristic features show through the family resemblance of Dewhurst's Colombian 4–8–0s; from above downwards, Kitson's and Berlin's lighter 3ft gauge engines for the Pacifico and Baldwin's and Berlin's metre-gauge ones for the Norte. The heavier 3ft gauge locomotives were only slightly smaller than the metre-gauge ones*

To reach further into the interior of Colombia the main traffic artery was the Magdalena river. On the left, west, bank of the river was the FC de Tolima, laid with 55lb/yd rails and with stronger bridges than the Pacifico. The maximum gradient was 1 in 30 with curves of 197ft radius. For this line six of the larger 3ft-gauge engines (216) were built by Baldwin soon after the smaller ones. They had a 12

ton axle load compared to $10\frac{1}{2}$ on the Pacific, and were correspondingly heavier and more powerful. Some virtually identical locomotives (217) were supplied by Baldwin to the Cundinamarca Railway.

The Central Northern Railway, FC del Norte, was one of the, then, metre-gauge lines radiating from Bogota, high in the mountains east of the Magdalena. It was laid with 55lb/yd rails, had grades up to 1 in 33 and 213ft radius curves. The 4–8–0s for this line were a little larger than the heavier 3ft gauge ones; some were built by Baldwin (218), by Berlin (219) and by Haine St Pierre (220), who built four in January and five in November, 1926 (Fig 74); two of four were to be oil burners and two three-cylinder engines (221), but it is not clear if the two variants from the two-cylinder coal-burning sort were independent or overlapped; one might have been a three-cylinder oil burner.

On the Pacifico the smaller 4–8–0s hauled 162 tons up 1 in 25, with some pitches at 1 in 23½, at a mean speed of 7½mph; 174 tons up 17 miles of 1 in 33, with pitches at 1 in 30, at 10mph; 365 tons up 20 miles of almost continuous 1 in 50 also at 10mph. It was noted that the Dewhurst engines accelerated on the curves, showing that the compensation was more than sufficient; the resistance due to curvature of these 4–8–0s was less than that of earlier loco-motives.

Baldwin also built some larger 3ft-gauge 4–8–0s for the Ambalema–Ibaque Railway (222), a little heavier than those for the Pacifico.

Some 4–8–0s were supplied to the Pacifico in 1927 by the Skoda Works, of Plzen, Czechoslovakia (223) (Fig 74) and Berlin built wood-burning ones (224) for the Caldas Railway.

The larger 3ft-gauge 4–8–0s were supplied by Skoda to the Girardot Railway (225). The Girardot had for long been one of the nationalised railways and connected the river port of that name on the Magdalena to Facatativa on the Cundinamarca Rail-way leading to Bogota. The Girardot rises from about 1,065ft to about 8,955ft in 78 miles, but with most of the climb, some 5,800ft in 33 miles, averag-ing 1 in 30·5. The maximum gradient was 1 in 25 and the minimum curve radius 260ft.

By contrast the FC La Dorada, the Dorada Rail-way, then operated by a British company, was easily graded with 12 miles of 1 in 50 and 260ft minimum curves. It lies on the west bank of the Magdalena, by-passing some rapids. The Dorada Railway had some 3ft-gauge 4–8–0s (226) from Hawthorn, Leslie in 1928.

The Dorada Railway was extended to make a junction at Ambalema with the Ambalema–Ibague

Fig 74 *Here too the builders' national details show clearly; Skoda's engine for the Pacifico (above) and Haine St Pierre's for the Norte*

and that joined the Tolima at Ibague; the Tolima connected with the Tolima–Huila–Caqueta and, later, when the Magdalena was bridged near Tolima and Girardot, with the Girardot, forming an extensive system of 3ft 0in gauge lines. Later, too, it was extended downstream to Puerto Berrio whence a line extends over the mountains to Caldas and up the Cauca valley to join the Pacifico. The Cauca was second in importance only to the Magdalena, of which it is the largest tributary.

About this time some 4–8–0s were supplied to Colombia by Les Ateliers Metallurgiques of Tubize, Belgium (227). The author has not traced how many or to which railways this builder sent the 4–8–0s.

Twenty-eight of these locomotives were in service in the latter part of 1957, built in five different works in five countries, Belgium, Britain, Czechoslovakia, Germany, and the USA, namely by Baldwin, Berlin, Haine St Pierre, Hawthorn, Leslie, and Skoda. They were then Nos 69-96, but some had been renumbered, and dated from 1926 to 1929. Two of the Berlin 4–8–0s were used in the late 1960s for making a film, although one had been withdrawn for some years and had one bogie axle missing due to 'cannibalisation', despite which it ran over fifty miles to reach the venue of the shooting! It was then scrapped, but the other returned to service.

As many railways in Colombia used 4–8–0s as did in Argentina, but the number of locomotives was smaller and the railways were not all independent. Moreover, all the 4–8–0s were of a single family, if of three sizes and several varieties.

Conclusion

The 4–8–0 was used less extensively in South America than in Africa, but in some respects there was more and in others less variation. The difference is in the occurrence of broad gauge and in the varied topography of different parts of South America. The broad-gauge lines in Argentina have few steep gradients, but train loads are heavy. In the Argentine locomotives were mostly British in origin. In the Andes the railways have gradients that for combined length and steepness are without parallel, yet the 4–8–0 filled a need there also, but the standard-gauge locomotives were mostly American. On the narrow gauge internationalism could hardly have gone further.

Some of the locomotives described are in service at the time of writing and likely to remain so for a time, so the 4–8–0 has been in service in South America longer than in Europe and for nearly as long as in Africa, but the number of engines was less than in either, probably nearly 400 all told.

The four countries named above are thought to be the only ones in South America that used 4–8–0s. The author has found no record of them in Bolivia, Chile, Ecuador, Paraguay, or Venezuela, or in the British, Dutch, or French colonial territories. In mid 1935 the Central Uruguay Railway received designs from Beyer, Peacock for the conversion of some 2–8–0s to 4–8–0s; P. C. Dewhurst had moved from Colombia to Uruguay! But was the conversion carried out?

CHAPTER 5

AUSTRALASIA

SECTION 13

(a) The Antipodes

AUSTRALIA has been a single political entity for most of the period covered by this chapter, but is divided into six states, each with a measure of autonomy. The railways in those states were partly developed before the Commonwealth came into being and largely independently of one another. New Zealand is politically distinct from Australia, but there is some co-operation between the railways of the two countries.

The railways in the six states on the Australian mainland form a connected system, but each has its own standards, track and loading gauges, as has the Commonwealth for its railways; several states have two or three gauges. The railway pioneers in Australia were nothing if not individualistic and the locomotive engineers likewise. New Zealand, too, went its own way.

Besides the main State or Government railway systems, there were a few privately owned railways of some importance. In most cases the railways were built to develop the land and were built cheaply with steep gradients, sharp curves, light track, and relatively weak bridges, many of timber construction. Some of the country is very rough indeed.

Neither New South Wales nor Victoria used 4–8–0s, but they ran on the state-owned railways of Queensland, South Australia, Tasmania, and Western Australia and on the narrow-gauge lines of the Commonwealth Railways. They were used by the private Emu Bay Railway in Tasmania and the former Midland Railway of Western Australia.

All the locomotives to be dealt with were built for the 3ft 6in gauge, but some on one railway achieved the rare distinction for a narrow-gauge class of being rebuilt for broad gauge and later converted back to narrow.

(b) New Zealand

New Zealand was first in the field and only one railway, the New Zealand Government Railways, is involved. New Zealand is mountainous, thinly populated and, over seventy years ago, was little industrialised. The railways were lightly built and had a very small loading gauge for 3ft 6in rail gauge.

The first 4–8–0s were ordered just before the turn of the century, four from Sharp, Stewart (228) (Fig 75) and one from the railway's Addington workshops. Statements conflict as to which were first to be built in 1899, but the Addington engine was the first to enter service. Beyer, Peacock prepared a design for a 4–8–0 for the NZGR late in 1897 so the idea of using that type must have been expressed some time before that. Five more were turned out from Addington between 1901 and 1903 (229). The design of these Class B engines was due to G. A. Pearson, chief draughtsman, working to the instruction of the locomotive superintendent, T. F. Rotheram, who soon afterwards moved to Western Australia. The first five had low running plates and the second five high ones. They had Walschaerts valve gear and piston valves, probably the first locomotives in the world to combine these features. They hauled 600 tons, later increased to 660, on easy grades, despite their 8·2 ton axle load, and 220 tons on the hilly line north of Dunedin. The NZGR rebuilt two of the first five as 4–6–4T tank engines in 1902 and one in 1943, the latter after some modifications. The first batch had the leading coupled wheels with blind tyres, but later the second and third coupled axles had wheels with no flanges. Two of the second lot had the engine wheelbase modified, the first and fourth coupled axles being 1ft closer together and the distance from bogie to leading coupled axle 6in longer.

Fig 75 *Sharp, Stewart's B class of 1899 for the New Zealand Government Railways with low running plate and sand boxes*

Between 1924 and 1929 five Bs were superheated (230) and four received larger boilers with wide fireboxes in 1929, 1935, and 1948. Some were adapted for shunting between 1928 and 1931, receiving a lower tender with a cab. Three were in service in 1956.

In 1911, Addington began to deliver engines of Class Ba, completing ten by 1913. They were to the design of A. L. Beattie and were superheated (231) (Fig 76). They were a little heavier than Class B. There were many changes over the years and all were converted for shunting, with tender cabs, between 1927 and 1936. In 1928 and 1929 two received larger boilers (232) and three already converted as shunters received such boilers in 1948 and 1949. The boiler centre line was raised from 6ft 3in to 7ft 4in for the wide firebox boilers, to get sufficient depth. Five had the original type of boiler in 1956. Classes B and Ba were for service in the South Island.

An order was placed with A. & G. Price, of Thames, NZ, for twenty 4–8–0s of Class Bb in 1914; these were to the design of H. H. Jackson and

were for service in the North Island (233). The order was increased to thirty and all were built between 1915 and 1918. All were modified for shunting with cab tenders between 1932 and 1938 and all still active in the middle 1950s. As built, the Bbs were rated to haul 700 tons on the level.

The New Zealand railways had only a small portion of their locomotives without a leading bogie, but they did later prefer engines with a two- or four-wheeled trailing truck, almost essential when locomotives of higher power had to be squeezed into the restricted loading gauge; there was no room for an adequate firebox above the coupled wheels.

(c) Tasmania

Tasmania is a small island with a low population and parts of it are mountainous. It is the smallest Australian State. As well as good agricultural land and forest, there are minerals and to tap these railways were built through very rough country in the northwest of the island. Besides the state-owned

Fig 76 *Addington's Ba class for the New Zealand Government Railways originally had wedge-shaped buffer beams; the B and Bb classes had straight ones.* (New Zealand Railways Publicity photograph)

F

Fig 77 The Emu Bay Railway's 4–8–0s had a distinctly Scottish appearance

Tasmanian Government Railways, there is a private company, the Emu Bay Railway, with a fairy heavy goods traffic to be hauled over severe grades. For this line Dübs built three 4–8–0s in 1900, a repeat delivery of one being made by North British in 1911. They were larger than those for New Zealand and had a distinctly Scottish aspect (234) (Fig 77), which is natural as David Jones of the Highland Railway was consulting engineer to the Emu Bay. Two of them were serviceable in the 1960s.

The Emu Bay's line has a ruling grade of 1 in 40, but there are some lengths of 1 in 33 and curvature is sharp and continuous.

One of these locomotives was involved in a stirring incident in 1912. Following an accident in the mines at Mount Lyell, rescue equipment was sent for from the mainland. The ship reached Burnie at dawn on 15 October; a 4–8–0 and one coach set off over the Emu Bay line to Zeehan and on over the Government line to Strahan; the last stage was over the Mount Lyell Railway's line to Queenstown. It is 88 miles from Burnie to Zeehan, about half as much more on to Strahan and $21\frac{1}{2}$ up to Queenstown, including over 4 miles of rack needing special locomotives. The run was made in five hours less than the schedule time. In Tasmania, as elsewhere, railwaymen rise to the occasion when life is at stake.

The Tasmanian Government Railways did not have any 4–8–0s of their own design, though such were considered in 1902, when Beyer, Peacock prepared two slightly different designs for them. They acquired some secondhand in 1921 from the South Australian Railways, which then no longer needed all their 3ft 6in-gauge locomotives (235) (Fig 78).

Fig 78 A South Australian Railways T class after being sold to the Tasmanian Government Railways and fitted with side buffers instead of centre buffer-couplers

Amongst other changes were the substitution of screw couplings and side buffers for central buffer-couplers and of vacuum for compressed air brakes. The TGR found these engines useful as it had them reboiled and superheated between 1927 and 1931 and all six were in service as late as 1950. All had been withdrawn by 1962 after some 750,000 miles each. They were rated to haul 170 tons on 1 in 40.

SECTION 14

THE AUSTRALIAN MAINLAND

Western Australia is the largest state in Australia, but has the smallest population of any on the mainland. The railways were inexpensively constructed. The rather sparse traffic could be handled economically only by running few, heavy trains over light track. Movement of the seasonal wheat crop taxed their resources to the limit.

These facts and the arrival of T. F. Rotheram, who had initiated the 4–8–0 design in New Zealand, make it no wonder that the type was introduced to the WAGR; Dübs built fifteen in 1901-2 (236) (Fig 79) and North British built twelve in 1911, two being superheated (237). Thirty saturated engines followed from North British in 1913-14. The Class F was for long the heaviest WAGR engine and was rated to haul 275 tons on 1 in 50. All but four were fitted with superheaters at Midland workshops in 1924 and 1925; about half had 18in and half 17in cylinders with 175lb/sq in boiler pressure.

There was until 1963 a company-owned line, the Midland Railway of Western Australia, running northwards from Midland Junction to rejoin the Government railway near Geraldton. This railway

had two 4–8–0 locomotives, Class D (238), built by Baldwin in 1920. The trailing and intermediate coupled wheels had blind tyres.

Both Queensland and South Australia introduced the 4–8–0 in 1903. The South Australian Railways had many locomotives built in Australia, some in their workshops at Islington and some by builders. The original 4–8–0s were introduced in the Peterborough division of the SAR when the 3ft 6in-gauge line was built to the New South Wales border to connect with the Silverton Tramway serving the mining area round Broken Hill. The 'Tramway' was so called for legal reasons, but was a railway. The Broken Hill mines provided the traffic that the T class engines (239) (Fig 78) were built to haul. They handled 525 tons on banks of 1 in 75. On this route they were the main motive power until the arrival of Garratts during and after the second world war. The T class soon spread to other SAR 3ft 6in-gauge lines. Besides four engines built at Islington there were thirty-four built by James Martin & Co, of Gawler, SA, in batches from 1904 to 1913, and forty by Walkers Ltd, of Maryborough, Queensland (240) in 1913, but some did not enter service until 1917. Some were ballasted to give 3·7 tons more adhesive weight.

By 1922 seventy-two Ts were in service on the SAR, six having been sold to Tasmania, but traffic was declining on the 3ft 6in gauge and in that year five surplus Ts were converted at Islington to Class TX for the 5ft 3in gauge (241). After over twenty-five years as broad-gauge engines they were reconverted to narrow gauge in 1949. The last T was withdrawn in June, 1970, but one had been transferred in that year to the Silverton Tramway.

The SAR converted some of its 3ft 6in-gauge lines to 5ft 3in gauge, particularly in the southeast of the

Fig 79 *Dübs F class for the Western Australian Government Railways of 1902*

Fig 80 *A C16 of the Queensland Railways of 1903; one was the first locomotive built at the new Islington workshops*

Fig 81 *A C17 of the Queensland Railways of 1919, a superheated and improved version of the C16*

state adjoining Victoria, which uses 5ft 3in gauge. Now the uniform gauge project for a direct line from Sydney to Perth has replaced the 3ft 6in-gauge route from Broken Hill to Port Pirie by one of 4ft 8½in gauge.

In Queensland the first 4–8–0, Class C16, was built in 1903 in the Queensland Railway workshops at Ipswich, then newly built, and this was the first new locomotive to be built there. The C indicates four coupled axles and 16 is the cylinder diameter in inches. Over a number of years 152 C16s were built, fifty-one at Ipswich (242), forty-one by Evans, Anderson, Phelan & Co of Brisbane, forty-five by Walkers, and fifteen by the Toowoomba Foundry, all in Queensland; evidently a successful design! They were designed by the CME, G. B. Nutt, to burn a semi-bituminous coal mined locally (Fig 80), and could run round a 3½ chain curve, but those on the line for which they were intended, were of 4 chains minimum.

Some built as saturated steam engines were later superheated (243).

In 1914 a new design of 4–8–0 was brought out by the CME, C. E. Pemberton, the C18, and they were built at Ipswich as saturated engines (244), but later they were superheated (245). They were the first built for the QR with piston valves. They were

larger than the C16s and were regarded as passenger, not goods, engines and were intended for the mail trains from Brisbane to Wallangara, for Sydney, which had to climb to Toowoomba, including some 1,200ft in fifteen miles or so, with 1 in 50 maximum grades and 5 chain curves; up this they maintained 20mph with 230 to 240 tons. The first was Ipswich works No 69 and was built in six weeks, in time for exhibition on QR's jubilee.

The superheating of the three C18s led to the design of superheated versions of both classes; no more C18s were built and in 1934 all were rebuilt as CC19 (246), similar to the later Class C19. Probably the outbreak and duration of the first world war caused the railway to eschew new designs.

In 1919, there appeared the first C17 (247) (Fig 81), a modernised, superheated version of the C16 which became the most numerous class of 4–8–0 in Australia. They were built for a number of years and the later ones had a boiler pressure of 175 instead of 160lb/sq in (248). Besides 16 built at Ipswich, one of which was works No 100, Evans, Anderson, Phelan & Co built 28, and 138 were obtained from Walkers (in fact Walkers built 214 4–8–0s, their total steam locomotives being 557, a remarkably high proportion of 4–8–0s). These engines were due to C. E. Pemberton and his assistants, J. H. Rees

Fig 82 *The larger C19 of the Queensland Railways first built in 1922; the C18 of 1914 was similar in appearance*

and R. J. Chalmers. The latter became CME and in 1927 ordered twenty-five C17s from Armstrong, Whitworth (249). These were shipped fully erected. Twenty were built in 1948/49 by the Clyde Engineering Company, of Granville, NSW (250). The number of these locomotives is testimony enough to their appreciation by the Queensland Railways.

The QR's last 4-8-0 class was the C19 (251) (Fig 82), the first being built at Ipswich in 1922, and ten completed by 1923. Six, with improvements (252), were built by Walkers in 1934 and Ipswich built another ten.

The total number of 4-8-0s built for Queensland, 408, was far larger than that for any other railway outside Europe, except the South African Railways, which had nearly as many built new, but not all originally for one railway. In Europe a large part of the RENFE's total was made up of those built for a number of railways: the MZA had ordered 408, but received only 338 before becoming part of the RENFE. Four QR 4-8-0s are preserved.

One other railway in Australia used 4-8-0s, namely the Commonwealth Railways on the 3ft 6in-gauge Central Australia line. This was completed to Alice Springs in August 1929, but fourteen 4-8-0s had been built in 1924 and eight in 1926, entering service in 1925 and 1927 on the southern part of the line, which was built first. They all came from Thompson & Company, of Castlemaine, Victoria (253). They were similar to the Queensland C17,

but with different buffing and draw gear; the QR use buffers and screw couplings and the Commonwealth narrow-gauge lines use central buffer-couplers. Some of them were in service well into the 1960s; the opening of the standard-gauge line by-passing the difficult part of the old route, curtailed their activities.

During the second world war much increased traffic necessitated more locomotives and in 1942 four 4-8-0s were borrowed from the SAR and eleven from the QR, all being returned the following year.

Conclusion

This brings to an end the story of the 4-8-0 in Australasia, where it played a considerable part in the motive power picture at times and a dominant part on some railways. It was built there for about fifty years and imported, the total number, about 630, being more than in South America and fewer than in Africa. In relation to the population served the number was higher than elsewhere. Whilst less obvious, because so many locomotives were locally designed, there does seem to be some influence from the Cape 7th class, which was established and well known when the first 4-8-0 was designed 'down under'. Apart from constructional features, each railway imparted a characteristic appearance to its engines, yet in essentials there was similarity between them.

CHAPTER 6

ASIA

SECTION 15

(a) East of Suez

THE railways of Asia are divided into large and small separate systems of varied characteristics, of different gauges, and of various standards for heavy, medium, and light axle loads. As far as the 4–8–0 is concerned, only three countries come into the picture, India, Ceylon, and China. In the first-named several railways were involved; most of them penetrated mountainous country. In other countries, where the type might be expected to have been used, the author has found no record of it; Burma for example, which is mountainous and where railways were Indian in character. Nor was it adopted in Thailand (Siam) or Malaya, in the former Dutch East Indies, or in Japan, where the mountainous terrain could have led to its use.

The majority of the 4–8–0s used in Asia were of British design and construction, the only large exception being those from Hungary.

(b) India

In India, which, for the period covered, includes what is at the time of writing Pakistan, the 4–8–0 was not used on the predominant broad gauge, but only on the important secondary metre-gauge system and the much less extensive 2ft 6in-gauge railways.

In early days, Indian railways were nearly as individualistic as in the United Kingdom and the USA in locomotive design; it was found that this caused difficulty when locomotives were drafted from one line to another for famine relief, military needs, or any other reason. This led to a measure of standardisation and a 'standards committee' was set up to design standard locomotives for the broad and metre gauges. Many were based on existing locomotives, but amongst the metre-gauge ones issued in 1903

was a new design, a 4–8–0 tender engine (254) (Fig 83).

Whilst details were settled to suit the conditions on Indian metre–gauge lines, it is probable that the members of the committee were aware of and influenced by the numerous 4–8–0s already built for 3ft 6in gauge in Africa.

All the metre-gauge 4–8–0s for India were based on this standard design, but none followed it in all respects. Soon after it was promulgated a change made in loading rules permitted an engine of this weight to have a wheelbase shorter than the standard. Before the issue of a revised standard in 1910 most engines were so built. The new standard changed the coupled and total engine wheelbases to 12ft 0in and 21ft 3in instead of 14ft 3in and 24ft 4½in, that is practically to those of the Cape 7th class.

The first line to order the new type was the Eastern Bengal Railway, which obtained five (255) (Fig 84) from North British in 1904. These were followed by ten for the Assam Bengal Railway (256) (Fig 85) also from North British and delivered in 1906. They were later given superheaters in the railway's workshops probably using imported material, perhaps new boilers (257). Beyer, Peacock prepared a design of a similar engine for this railway late in 1905.

By 1907 the Southern Mahratta Railway had in service five similar engines from North British (258). The Assam Railway & Trading Company bought six 4–8–0s built by Nasmyth, Wilson in 1908 (259). They were to be resold later to the ABR, being used on the notorious hill section of its main line, with long lengths of 1 in 37 on which they hauled 175 tons. They were hired to the ABR until it could raise the funds for purchase. About two years later Vulcan Foundry began to build 4–8–0s for the Madras

THE ENGINEERING STANDARDS COMMITTEE

HEAVY GOODS STANDARD ENGINE & TENDER (MASTODON)

FOR

METRE GAUGE

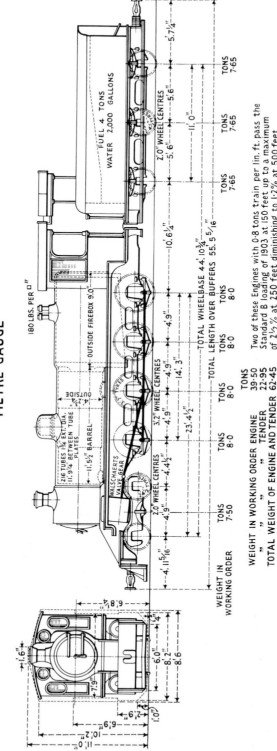

180 LBS. PER □"

216 TUBES 1¾ EXT. DIA. 11.9/4 BETWEEN TUBE PLATES — 11'.5½" BARREL — OUTSIDE FIREBOX 9'.0" — OUTSIDE 4'.2¼" — WALSCHAERTS VALVE GEAR

FUEL 4 TONS — WATER 2,000 GALLONS

WEIGHT IN WORKING ORDER

TONS 7.50	TONS 8.0	TONS 8.0	TONS 8.0	TONS 7.65	TONS 7.65	TONS 7.65	TONS 7.65

4'.11.5/16" — 2'.0" WHEEL CENTRES — 4'.9" — 4'.4½" — 3'.2" WHEEL CENTRES — 4'.9" — 4'.9" — 4'.9" — 14'.3" — 23'.4½" — 10'.6¼" — 2'.0" WHEEL CENTRES — 5'.6" — 5'.6" — 11'.0" — 5'.7¼" — 1'.0"

— TOTAL WHEELBASE 44'.10¾" — TOTAL LENGTH OVER BUFFERS 55'.5.5/16" —

8'.9" — 4" — 6'.0" — 8'.2" — 8'.6" — 1'.6" — 7'.9" — 6'.9" — 2'.3" — 1'.0" — 6'.9" — 10'.2" — 11'.0"

TONS
WEIGHT IN WORKING ORDER ENGINE ... 39·50
" " " TENDER ... 22·95
TOTAL WEIGHT OF ENGINE AND TENDER ... 62·45

Two of these Engines with 0·8 tons train per lin. ft. pass the Standard B loading of 1903 at 150 feet up to a maximum of 2½ % at 250 feet diminishing to 1·2% at 500 feet

GAUGE	CYLINDER DIA. STROKE	COUPLED WHEELS DIA.	BOILER LBS. PER SQ. IN.	HEATING SURFACE SQUARE FEET			GRATE AREA SQ. FT.	WEIGHT IN WORKING ORDER			WEIGHT ON COUPLED WHEELS	TRACTIVE FORCE	ADHESIVE WEIGHT ÷ TRACTIVE FORCE (FACTOR OF ADHESION)
				TUBES	FIREBOX	TOTAL		ENGINE	TENDER	TOTAL			
METRE	16"×22"	3'.7"	180	1,164·8	126·2	1,291	17·5	39·50T.	22·95T.	62·45TNS.	32 TONS	17,682 LBS @ 75%.B.P.	4·05
												21,218 ,, ,, 90% ,,	3·38

Fig 83 *Facsimile of Plate 5 in Report No 5 issued by The Engineering Standards Committee, which became The British Engineering Standards Association and, later, the British Standards Institution. This design was the basis of all the Indian metre gauge 4-8-0s. (Reproduced by courtesy of the British Standards Institution)*

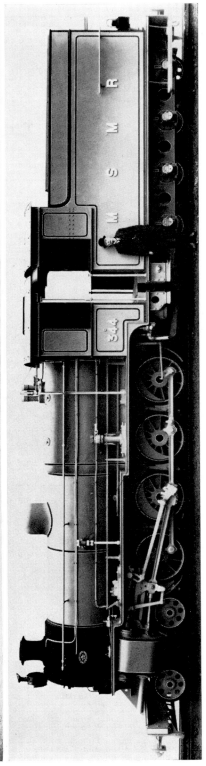

(top)   Fig 84   *The Eastern Bengal Railway's 4–8–0s were the first built for India and show the long coupled wheelbase*
(middle)   Fig 85   *The Assam Bengal Railway's 4–8–0s had the shorter coupled wheelbase of the revised standard*
(bottom)   Fig 86   *The Madras & Southern Mahratta Railway's 4–8–0s had a still shorter engine wheelbase, as shown by this one built in 1920*

& Southern Mahratta Railway, as the SMR had become by amalgamation with the Madras Railway, starting with two lots of five (260) in 1910 and 1911 followed by two lots of five and seven in 1912 and 1913, which may have had coupled wheels 4ft 0in in diameter instead of 3ft 7in (261).

Most of these 4–8–0s had a wheelbase shorter than the 1903 standard and some were shorter than the 1910 standard. Those for the AR & T CO were to the revised standard, but the M & SM ones were 9in shorter between bogie and leading coupled wheels. Despite nearly identical boilers the different axle spacing caused differences in weight distribution. The AR & T engines had unusual tenders, able to hold 7½ tons of coal and 2,000 gallons of water, but if the tank was full only three tons of coal were allowed and with the bunker full only 1,000 gallons; the total of coal and water was not to exceed 12 tons. This must have posed some problems for the staff. The standard metre-gauge tender held 4 tons and 2,000 gallons.

In 1914 Nasmyth, Wilson built ten 4–8–0s for the Nizam's Guaranteed State Railway (262), the first of a series of deliveries in 1915/16 and 1920, the last having been delayed by the war from an intended 1917 building date, and again in 1920, the numbers being four, four and five respectively. The 1920 ones were superheated.

As mentioned in Section 10 (c) four 4–8–0s (263) being built for the Nizam's Railway by Nasmyth, Wilson during the 1914–18 war were sent to German East Africa instead; it is not known to the author if they remained in Africa or later reached India, but the former seems more probable.

The 4–8–0s sent from India to East Africa were also built by Nasmyth, Wilson perhaps some of those for the AR & T, or the Nizam's. These probably returned to India.

In 1918 and 1919 the M & SM ordered six and then thirty-two superheated 4–8–0s from North British (264), then in 1921 Vulcan Foundry built four superheated 4–8–0s for the ABR (265) and five for the Mysore State Railway in 1922 (266); five for the Nizam's followed in 1923 from Nasmyth, Wilson (267). A modernised, superheated version was supplied to the South Indian Railway and to the M & SM, some for the former by Vulcan Foundry and for the latter by Bagnall in 1924 or 1925. The SIR engines had six-wheeled tenders (268) and those for the M & SM (269) (Fig 86) eight-wheeled non-bogie ones. On the SIR the 4–8–0s were used to work 550 gross tons over a hilly section where earlier 4–6–0s could not take through a full load. A small railway, the Bengal–Dooars, received a couple of 4–8–0s (270) from Nasmyth, Wilson in 1928. In 1936 the Rheinische Metallwaaren & Maschinen-fabrik, of Düsseldorf, built some 4–8–0s for the Jamnagar–Dwarka Railway (271), which had six-wheeled tenders. Several of these railways had the same consulting engineers, Rendel, Palmer & Tritton, or their predecessors Rendel & Robertson.

In India 4–8–0s were used on several 2ft 6in-gauge lines, including the Great Indian Peninsula Railway (272) and perhaps the Bengal Nagpur Railway (273). The GIP engines were later transferred to the Dholpur Railway and were running there in 1968; they had been built in 1925 and 1926 by Hanomag, who also supplied 4–8–0s to the Bhavnagar State Railway (274) (Fig 87) at about that time, as did Bagnall (275) ten years later. The author has not found out who supplied those for the BNR and is not convinced that they really were 4–8–0s.

Fig 87 *The Bhavnagar State Railway's 2ft 6in gauge 4–8–0s were much like those for the Sierra Leone Government Railway. Compare Fig 60*

Fig 88 *A heavy 4–8–0 for the Ceylon Government Railway*

These 2ft 6in-gauge lines were mainly in difficult country and were built at minimum cost with sharp curves, steep grades, and light track. The 4–8–0s were rather like those for the Sierra Leone Government Railway in Africa.

It will be seen that though used on a relatively small scale, the 4–8–0 has served India for sixty-five years and may do so for some years to come.

(c) Ceylon and China

Ceylon, as regards railways, is more mountainous than India, but the busiest lines there had a smaller traffic than on a number of Indian ones such as the East Indian or those up the 'Ghats' on the routes inland from Bombay. The gauge of all main lines in Ceylon is 5ft 6in. The Kadugannawa incline on the main line from Colombo to Kandy and Nuwara Eliya, has 12 miles of 1 in 45 with 10 chain curves in the 13 miles from Rabukkana to Kadugannawa and trains were allowed sixty minutes for the climb. To work up this bank, Kitson built five 4–8–0s. With another smaller locomotive the load was 350 tons, apportioned in a ratio of about 2 to 1. Two of them (276) (Fig 88) built in 1911, used dried steam and three (277) in 1913 were superheated. The drive was on the third coupled axle and the leading

Fig 89 *A light 4–8–0 of the Ceylon Government Railway*

Fig 90 *A lightweight 4–8–0 for the Hangchow–Kiangshan Railway*

coupled wheels had blind tyres. They were rather ungainly looking engines, but they did the job, for another was ordered from Kitson in 1921. It is noteworthy that the consulting engineers were Gregory, Eyles, and Waring: Gregory & Eyles had been consulting engineers for the Cape 7th and 8th classes in 1892 and 1903. The two 1911 engines were given new superheated boilers in due course.

Some lines in Ceylon were lightly built and laid with 45lb/yd rails, more like a narrow- than a broad-gauge line, so the locomotive axle loads had to be kept down. In 1928 Hunslet built two 4–8–0s with an axle load of 9 tons (278) (Fig 89). Two more followed in each of the years 1929 and 1930. Three similar engines were ordered from Bagnall in 1939 and six with detail improvements (279) in 1951.

In China the situation was similar to that in Ceylon, but events took place in the reverse order. In 1933 Hunslet built six 4–8–0s with light axle load for the Hangchow–Kiangshan Railway (280) (Fig 90). They were lighter than those for Ceylon, but had a distinct resemblance to them: they were built partly to metric dimensions. These, too, gave satisfaction as four more were ordered in 1936. An unusual feature was the fitting of two couplers at different heights.

A score or so years later a number of heavier main-line locomotives were built for China by Mavag. These were Hungarian locomotives of MAV class 424 similar to those built also for the USSR, Jugoslavia, and Slovakia, with suitable modifications to the couplings and so on (281). It is possible that more of them may have been built in China, but the author has no definite information on this point.

Conclusion

In Asia, India was the first country to introduce the 4–8–0, but for both Ceylon and China such engines were built much more recently. The information available makes it difficult to estimate the number that were used in Asia, but it was probably far fewer than, perhaps only half, that for South America, unless the Chinese had many more than the author thinks is the case.

The type was supplied to Asia for some fifty years and appreciable numbers are still at work there. It was the suitability of the 4–8–0 for hill and mountain climbing and for use on light track that made it accepted by the various railways and by most well enough regarded to be ordered again as the need arose.

This must also be the end of this account of the 4–8–0 throughout the world. Its building went on for a century and some specimens are still doing useful work. A few are preserved for posterity. It was much less numerous than some other types, but there were nearly 5,000 of them of many varieties, large and small, all built to fill a need on the railway, where and when it occurred. In some countries it was a very important type of locomotive making a major contribution to the haulage of both passenger and goods trains. A large proportion of 4–8–0s were of British design and construction and were a credit to the once numerous firms of locomotive builders as well as to the designers on the railways and the consulting engineers. Nearly all, everywhere, were good, sound, workmanlike jobs and some were truly inspired creations.

ACKNOWLEDGEMENTS

THE author wishes to express his thanks to many people, firms, railways and other organisations, without whose help the information contained in this book would have been much less complete.

In addition to those whose names appear in the credits for photographs, the author wishes particularly to mention the following:
John Alcock, J. W. Bulman, G. W. Carpenter, J. M. Doherty, M. W. Faville sen, L. T. George, A. Giesl–Gieslingen, J. Gillieaux, G. Horsman, V. M. Marshall, M. F. Nicolson, D. Patrick, C. Primatesta, W. Saliger, E. Schmiege, H. Smedley, W. G. F. Thorley, J. Vittone, R. J. Walker, C. R. Webb, A. J. Webberley, J. H. White jun, F. H. Wood, G. K. Wood

LOCOMOTIVE BUILDERS AND THEIR SUCCESSORS
Société Alsacienne de Constructions Mécanique de Mulhouse; Astilleros Españoles, SA (Euskalduna); Sociedad Española de Construcciones Babcock & Wilcox; William Beardmore & Co Ltd; Breda Termomeccanica e Locomotive, SpA; La Brugeoise et Nivelles, SA; Clyde Engineering Co Pty Ltd; Société Franco-Belge de Materiel de Chemins de Fer; Ganz-Mávag; Hamjern A/S (Hamar); Hudswell Badger Ltd; Material y Construcciones, SA (Devis); Société MTE (Schneider, Le Creusot); Nohab; A. & G. Price Ltd; Thompsons (Castlemaine) Ltd; Thune-Eureka A/S; Walkers Limited

RAILWAYS
Bas Congo Katanga; Benguela; British Railways Board; Butte, Anaconda & Pacific; Central of New Jersey; Commonwealth; Delaware & Hudson; Duluth, Missabe & Iron Range; East African; Jamaica Railway Corporation; Lehigh Valley; Caminho de Ferro de Luanda; Missouri Pacific Lines; Caminho de Ferro de Moçamedes; Norfolk & Western; Österreichische Bundesbahnen; Penn Central Transportation Co; Rêde Ferroviaria Federal, SA, Estrada de Ferro Santos a Jundiai; Rêde Ferroviaria Federal SA, Sistema Regional Nordeste; South African; South Australian; Southern Pacific Transportation Co; Western Australian Government

ORGANISATIONS
Association du Musée Français du Chemin de Fer; Crown Agents for Overseas Governments and Administrations; Corporation of Glasgow Libraries Department; City of Liverpool Museums; Minnesota Historical Society; Railway and Locomotive History Society, Inc; The Science Museum

ILLUSTRATIONS

BIBLIOGRAPHY

American Locomotives, Alexander
Cavalcade of New Zealand Locomotives, Palmer & Stewart
A Century of Southern Pacific Steam Locomotives, Dunscombe
Chicago & North Western Steam Power, Knudsen
Die Entwicklung der Lokomotive, von Helmholtz and Staby
A Hunslet Hundred, Rolt
Iron Horses, Alexander
Iron Horses of the Santa Fé Trail
The Last Steam Locomotives of Western Europe, Ransome-Wallis
La Locomotiva a Vapore, Abate
La Locomotive Actuelle, Demoulin
Locomotive Panorama, Vol I, Cox
The Locomotives of Australia and New Zealand
Les Locomotives au Debut du XXe Siècle, Sauvage
Locomotive FS Italia
Les Locomotives Modernes, Meunier and Davallon
Locomotives of the Jersey Central
Locomotives of the New York Central Lines, Edson and May
La Locomotive à Vapeur, Chapelon
Locomotives à Vapeur de la SNCF
Lokomotivlära, Höjer
The Londonderry & Lough Swilly Railway, Patterson
La Machine Locomotive, Sauvage and Chapelon
New York Central's Early Power, Staufer
Railways of the Andes, Fawcett
Railways of Australia, Singleton and Burke
Railway Reminiscences of Three Continents, Vuillet
The Railways of Spain, Boag
Recent Locomotives
Russian Steam Locomotives, le Fleming and Price
Un Siècle (1840-1938) de Materiel et Traction sur

le Reseau d'Orleans, Villain
Steam on the Renfe, Marshall
Steam on the Sierra, Allen and Wheeler
The Steam Locomotive in America, Bruce
The Steam Locomotives of Eastern Europe, Durrant
The Story of the Baltimore & Ohio Railroad, Hungerford
Traité des Chemins de Fer (Locomotives), Moreau
Traité Pratique de la Machine Locomotive, Demoulin
Tratato Moderno di Materiale Mobili ed Esercizio delle Ferrovie, Tajani
Principal Results of Tests with Locomotive Type 2–4–0 M (In Russian)

WORKS OF REFERENCE
Locomotive Dictionary, 1906, 1912, 1916
Locomotive Cyclopaedia, 1922, 1927, 1938, 1947
Henschel Handbook, 1935

JOURNALS, ETC
Bulletins of the Railway and Locomotive Historical Society, Nos 22, 25, 42, 48, 55, 72, 75, 84, 90, 94, 96, 109, 116
Journal of the Institution of Locomotive Engineers
The New Zealand Railway Observer
Australian Railway Historical Society
British Standards Institution, Reports Nos 5 and 50
Stephenson Locomotive Society, *1970*

HOUSE JOURNALS
Baldwin Locomotives and *Records of Recent Construction*
Henschel Heft and *Henschel Review*
Hanomag Nachrichten and *Hanomag Journal*
Beyer, Peacock Quarterly Review

South African Railways & Harbours Magazine

PERIODICALS
The Engineer, Vols 54 (1882), 80 (1895), 82 (1896), 84 (1897), 85 (1898), 90 (1900), 94 (1902), 98 (1904), 108 (1909), 115 (1913), 118 (1914), 138 (1924), 140 (1925), 146 (1928), 157 (1934)
Engineering, Vols 33 (1882), 63 (1897), 64 (1897), 65 (1898), 90 (1910), 137 (1934)
Ferrocarriles y Tranvias
Génie Civil
Glasers Annalen
The Locomotive, Railway Carriage & Wagon Review, almost all years from 1899 to 1959, *1934*
Die Lokomotive
Modern Transport

Organ für die Fortschritte des Eisenbahnwesens
The *Railway Engineer*, 1892, 1898, 1907, 1909, 1910, 1911, 1914, 1917, 1919, 1920, 1922, 1923, 1924, 1925, 1928, 1929, 1933, 1934
The *Railway Gazette*, 1906, 1908, 1909, 1910*, 1911, 1912, 1913*, 1925, 1926*, 1927*, 1929*, 1933, 1934, *1935*, 1936
The *Railway Magazine*, 1919, and most years from 1924 to 1971, *1934*
Revue Générale des Chemins de Fer, 1907, 1910, 1911, *1935*
VDI Zeitschrift

* Special Numbers published in these years
Years in *italics* have items on the Chapelon locomotives

TABL

Serial No.	Date	Railway or Railroad	Builder	Cylinders dia x stroke inches	Coupled Wheels diameter ft	in	Boiler Pressure lb/sq in	Grate Area sq ft	Heating Surface Firebox sq ft	Tubes sq ft	Evaporative sq ft	Superheat Surf sq
1	1844	B & W	Hinkley	13½ x 20	3	0						
2	1855	B & O	Winans	22 x 22	3	7		25	125	945	1,070	—
4	1872	LV	Weatherly	20 x 26	4	1						
5	1880	LV	Weatherly	20 x 26	4	0	125	32	179	1,142	1,321	
6	1881	A & P	Rhode Island	20 x 26	4	2						
7	1882	CP	Sacramento	19 x 30	4	6	135	25·75	181·9	1,173·4	1,355·3	—
8	1882	CP	Cooke	20 x 30	4	6	135	25·75	181·9	1,173·4	1,355·3	—
9	1887	P & NY	Baldwin	20 x 24	4	2⅛	130	38·5		1,479		—
10	1887	BC	Schenectady	20 x 26	4	3	140	31·3	147·5	1,733·8	1,881·3	—
11	1889	SP	Schenectady	20 x 26	4	2	160					

TABL

Serial No.	Date	Railway or Railroad	Builder	Cylinders dia x stroke inches	Coupled Wheels diameter ft	in	Boiler Pressure lb/sq in	Grate Area sq ft	Heating Surface Firebox sq ft	Tubes sq ft	Evaporative sq ft	Superheat Surf sq
12	1891	SP	Schenectady	20 & 29 x 26	4	3	180					
13	1891	FE & MV	Schenectady	16 x 20	3	0	160	14·45	90	872·65	962·65	—
14	1891	GN	Brooks	20 x 26	4	7	180	24·6	182·1	2,026·3	2,208·4	
15	1892	IR & HB	Brooks	20 x 26	4	8	180	26·0*	189·35	2,107·75	2,297·1	—
16	1893	D & IR	Schenectady	22 x 26	4	6	170	34·45	189·7	2,212·5	2,402·2	
19	1895	SP	Schenectady	22 x 26	4	6	180					
20	1896	St L & A	Brooks	21 x 26	4	6	180	29·7		2,037		
21	1896	NP	Schenectady	23 & 34 x 30	4	7	200	35·0	206·5	2,721·6	2,943·4†	
22	1896	D & IR	Baldwin	22 x 26	4	6						
23	1897	BR & P	Brooks	21 x 26	4	7	180	30·0		2,121		
24	1897	GN	Brooks	21 x 34	4	7	210	35·2	235	3,047	3,282	
27	1898	BR & P	Brooks	20 x 26	4	7	200					
28	1898	GN	Brooks	19 x 32	4	7	200	35·2	219·5	2,624·1	2,843·6	—

*Also given as 31·6   †Including 15·3sq ft water tubes

TABL

Serial No.	Date	Railway or Railroad	Builder	Cylinders dia x stroke inches	Coupled Wheels diameter ft	in	Boiler Pressure lb/sq in	Grate Area sq ft	Heating Surface Firebox sq ft	Tubes sq ft	Evaporative sq ft	Superheat Surf sq
29	1899	C & EI	Schenectady	?21½ & 33 x 30	4	6					2,447	—
30	1899	CNJ	Brooks	21 x 32	4	7	200	82·8			3,168	
31	1899	DL & W	Brooks	21 x 32	4	6	200	82·4	218	2,950	3,168	
32	1899	IC	Brooks	23 x 30	4	9	210	37·5			3,494	—
33	1899	B & A	Schenectady	22 & 34 x 28	4	6						
34	1899	GN	Rogers	19 x 32	4	7	210	34·0	198	2,250	2,448	
36	1900	DL & W	Dickson	21 x 32	4	6	200	82·4	218	2,950	3,168	
37	1900	GN	Brooks	19 x 32	4	7	210	35·2			3,080	—
39	1900	BA & P	Schenectady	23 & 34 x 32	4	8	210				3,866	—
40	1901	St LIM & S	Alco	21 x 32	4	7	190	61·8*	272*‡	2,601*	2,873*	550
42	1906	N & W	Baldwin	21 x 30	4	8	200	44·5	157	2,783	2,940	—
43	1908	LT & W	Baldwin	22 x 26	4	8	200	33·4	200	3,124	3,324	—
44	1910	N & W	Baldwin	24 x 30	4	8	200	44·7	219	3,922	4,041	—
45	1933	D & H	Alco	†	5	3	500	75·8	1,026	2,325	3,351	1,076

†Triple expansion: one 20in, one 27½in and two 33in diameter, all 32in stroke   ‡Including thermic syphons and arch tube

Wheelbase				Weight in Working Order				Supplies		Remarks
Rigid in	Coupled ft in	Engine ft in	E & T ft in	Adhesive tons	Engine tons	Tender tons	E & T tons	Fuel tons	Water gallons	Remarks
					31.25					Existence doubtful Data approximate
0⅛	13 0⅛	23 2	46 9	38.6	45.4	24.0	69.4	3.55	2,145	
9	15 9	24 11½	53 1¾	47.35	54.9	28.1	83.0	5.35	2,500	} Tube heating
9	15 9	24 11½	53 1¾	47.35	54.9	28.1	83.0	5.35	2,500	surface inside
				39.1	50.1					
9	13 9	23 6	49 0		58.05			7.15	2,915	

[

Wheelbase				Weight in Working Order				Supplies		Remarks
Rigid in	Coupled ft in	Engine ft in	E & T ft in	Adhesive tons	Engine tons	Tender tons	E & T tons	Fuel tons	Water gallons	Remarks
				53.65	62.85					‡gallons of oil
11	10 2	18 0	39 0½	24.1	29.5	24.6	54.1	1,000‡	1,750	3ft gauge
8	15 6	25 1	52 1	58.95	69.65	38.4	108.05	7.15	3,335	Boiler pressure later lowered to 160lb/sq in
6	15 6	25 0	52 0	60.7	72.3	34.8	107.1	7.6	3,335	Grate area and heating surface approximate
6	15 6	25 4		62.0	75.4	32.65	108.05	5.8	2,700	
6	15 6	25 4		65.6	78.1					
8	15 8	25 5		66.1	78.1					
6	15 6	26 4	53 8	66.95	83.05	40.8	123.85	6.7	3,335	
				62.5	76.9					
8	15 8	25 5		64.8	77.5					
8	15 10	26 8	53 11	76.8	95.0	42.85	137.85	7.15	4,165	Boiler pressure later lowered to 180lb/sq in
					70.55					
	15 4	26 2	53 10	63.4	78.55	40.2	118.75	7.15	4,165	Boiler pressure later lowered to 180lb/sq in

[I

Wheelbase				Weight in Working Order				Supplies		Remarks
Rigid in	Coupled ft in	Engine ft in	E & T ft in	Adhesive tons	Engine tons	Tender tons	E & T tons	Fuel tons	Water gallons	Remarks
6	15 6	26 4		67.0	84.7					
				71.0	89.7					Cylinders later lined to 20in diameter
	15 0	25 9	50 4	74.1	91.5	49.0	140.5	8.9	4,165	Cyls later lined to 20in dia and pressure reduced
9	15 9	26 6	55 2	86.25	103.65	58.95	162.6		4,165	
	15 7	26 5								Pressure later lowered to 180lb/sq in
	15 0	25 9	50 4	74.1	91.5	49.0	140.5	8.9	4,165	
				66.95	81.25					Boiler pressure later lowered to 180lb/sq in
				74.5	96.65					
	15 6	26 4	60 6½★	81.9★	104.0★	72.0★	176.0★			★As later rebuilt by Missouri Pacific
6	15 6	26 5	53 7	73.9	88.9	51.7	140.6	8.35	4,165	
	16 0	26 0	56 10½	65.0	80.8	49.1	129.9	9.4	4,585	
0	16 0	27 1		95.2	116.55					
10	18 10	33 9	83 9	139.75	170.55	122.55	293.1	15.6	11,665	Water-tube firebox

G

4-8-0 TENDER LOCOMOTIVES

TABL

Serial No.	Date	Railway or Railroad	Builder	Cylinders dia x stroke inches	Coupled Wheels diameter ft	in	Boiler Pressure lb/sq in	Grate Area sq ft	Heating Surface Firebox sq ft	Tubes sq ft	Evaporative sq ft	Sup heat Surf sq
46	1901	JGR	Kitson	19½ x 24	3	10	180	24·25	127	1,285	1,412	—
47	1907	JGR	Baldwin	19 x 26	3	10	190	30	148	1,879	2,027	—
48	1914	JGR		19½ x 24	3	10	180	30	196	1,926	2,122	—
49	1920	JGR	Canadian	19 x 26	3	10	190	33·8	146·5	1,642	1,788.5	390
51	1936	JGR	Nasmyth Wilson	19 x 26	3	10	190	33·0	146	1,827	1,973	405
52	1944	JGR	Canadian	19 x 26	3	10	190	33·8			1,774·5	390
53	1924	N de M	Baldwin	28 x 28	5	7						
54	1935	N de M	Baldwin	28 x 28	5	7	200	66·7	299†	3,575	3,874	1,028

TABL

Serial No.	Date	Railway or Railroad	Builder	Cylinders dia x stroke inches	Coupled Wheels diameter ft	in	Boiler Pressure lb/sq in	Grate Area sq ft	Heating Surface Firebox sq ft	Tubes sq ft	Evaporative sq ft	Sup heat Surf sq
55	1902	RM	Ansaldo Breda	21¼ & 31½ x 26¾	4	7⅛	199	47·35	147·5†	1,773	1,920·5	—
56	1906	FS	OM	21¼ & 31½ x 26¾	4	7⅛	199	47·35	147·5†	1,956	2,103·5	—
57		FS		21¼ & 31½ x 26¾	4	7⅛	199	37·65			2,288·2	—
58	1905	L & LS	Hudswell Clarke	15½ x 22	3	9	170	15	115·9	889·6	1,004·5	—
59	1906	Minera	NBL	19 x 24	3	9	180	31	122	1,644	1,766*	—
60	1913	Minera	NBL	19 x 24	3	9	180	31			1,703	—
61	1907	PLM	Various	15 & 23⅝ x 25⅝	4	11	227	33·15	171·15†	2,489†	2,660·15†	—
62	1908	PLM	Various	15 & 23⅝ x 25⅝	4	11	227	33·15	171·15†	2,489·7†	2,660·85†	—
63	1909	PLM		15 & 23⅝ x 25⅝	4	11	227	33·15	171·15†	1,715·4†	1,886·55†	701

†Heating surfaces on fire side

TABL

Serial No.	Date	Railway or Railroad	Builder	Cylinders dia x stroke inches	Coupled Wheels diameter ft	in	Boiler Pressure lb/sq in	Grate Area sq ft	Heating Surface Firebox sq ft	Tubes sq ft	Evaporative sq ft	Sup heat Surf sq
65	1910	NSB	SLM	15 x 23⅝	4	5⅛	171	29·15	109·8	1,496·2	1,606·0	358
66	1912	NSB	Thune	15 x 23⅝	4	5⅛	171	29·15	109·8	1,467·1	1,576·9	358
67	1914	NSB	Thune	16⅛ x 23⅝	4	5⅛	171	32·3			1,787·4†	489
68	1919	NSB	Various	15⅜ & 23 x 23⅝	4	5⅛	185	29·15	108·7	1,495·1	1,603·8	358
69	1921	NSB	Various	16½ & 24¾ x 23⅝	4	5⅛	185	32·3	128·1	1,820·2	1,948·3	434
70	1915	Südbahn	Steg	24 x 25½	5	8½	199	48·1	173·3	2,173·2	2,346·5	811
71	1917	K-O	Steg	24 x 25½	5	8½	199	48·1	173·3	2,173·2	2,346·5	811
72	1923	OBB	Steg	22 x 28⅜	5	8½	213	48·0	173·3	2,173·2	2,346·5	809
73	1924	MAV	Mavag	23⅝ x 26	5	3¼	185	47·9	186·2	2,143·1	2,329·3	599
76	1925	PKP	Pierwsza	24¼ x 25½	5	8⅞	199	48·95	173·3	1,977·2	2,150·5	641
77		SZD		21¼ x 27½	5	7¾	185	64·6	198·6	2,596·1	2,794·7	1,029

†Heating surfaces on fire side

V

Wheelbase								Weight in Working Order				Supplies		Remarks
Rigid in	Coupled ft	Coupled in	Engine ft	Engine in	E & T ft	E & T in	Adhesive tons	Engine tons	Tender tons	E & T tons	Fuel tons	Water gallons	
3	12	9	23	0	46	10½	41·65	53·4	40·3	93·7	6	3,000	
9	12	9	23	0			49·0	62·0	33·8	95·8	5	3,000	Pressure later reduced to 180lb/sq in
3	12	9	23	0			47·6	60·5	40·3	100·8	6	3,000	Rebuild of 45
1	12	9	23	0	50	2	54·0	67·5	41·0	108·5	6·25	3,500	Semi-rigid wheelbase 8ft 8in
4	13	0	23	3	49	5	53·3	69·4	40·85	110·25	6	3,500	Semi-rigid wheelbase 8ft 8in
			22	8			53·5	67·4					Converted to burn oil in 1946
	18	0	30	10	67	5							
	18	0	30	10	67	5	102·7	128·6	75·5	204·1	2,920*	7,080	†Including 2 syphons *Gallons of oil

Wheelbase								Weight in Working Order				Supplies		
Rigid in	Coupled ft	Coupled in	Engine ft	Engine in	E & T ft	E & T in	Adhesive tons	Engine tons	Tender tons	E & T tons	Fuel tons	Water gallons	Remarks
11¾	14	11½	26	1⅜			54·75	73·25	33·0	106·25	4	2,860	2-cylinder compound
11¾	14	11½	26	5⅜			57·5	74·2	33·45	107·65	4	2,860	2-cylinder compound
11¾	14	11½	26	1⅜	48	5½	57·3	74·2	34·25	108·45	4·5	2,860	Rebuild of 55
	13	6	21	7½			28·0	37·0	21·4	58·4	4	1,500	3ft gauge
8			23	0	49	2	53·0	63·2	35·25	98·45	4·5	3,080	1 metre gauge *Also given as 1767
							53·0	63·2			4·5	3,080	1 metre gauge
9⅞	18	0½	30	4⅛			59·2	73·3	38·4	113·7	4·95	3,540	4-cylinder compound unbraked
9⅞	18	0½	30	4⅛			60·0	78·05	39·2	117·25	4·95	3,540	4-cylinder compound braked
9⅞	18	0½	30	4⅛									4-cylinder compound

I

Wheelbase								Weight in Working Order				Supplies		
Rigid in	Coupled ft	Coupled in	Engine ft	Engine in	E & T ft	E & T in	Adhesive tons	Engine tons	Tender tons	E & T tons	Fuel tons	Water gallons	Remarks
1⅞	16	4⅞	27	8⅝	49	8½	45·85	61·2	35·0	96·2	3·95	3,305	4-cylinder simple
1⅞	16	4⅞	27	8⅝	49	8½	46·75	63·4	35·0	98·4	3·95	3,305	4-cylinder simple
6⅜	16	6	27	9⅞	51	7¼	55·0	73·8	42·5	116·3	4·95	4,410	4-cylinder simple
1⅞	16	4⅞	27	8⅝	49	10⅝	47·8	67·7	{35·0 / 41·35}	{102·7 / 109·05}	{3·95 / 5·9}	{3,305 / 4,010}	4-cylinder compound
6⅜	16	6	27	9⅞	51	7¼	56·7	78·75	41·5	120·25	4·95	4,410	4-cylinder compound
1⅝	18	2½	31	3¼			57·5	83·55	57·1	140·65	7·4	5,950	
1⅝	18	2½	31	3¼	56	4⅛	59·0	84·8	54·6	139·4	6·9	5,950	
1⅝	18	2½	31	3¼			58·5	83·8	54·6	138·4	6·9	5,950	Lentz poppet valves
9¾	17	8⅝	31	2	56	10⅝	55·6	81·0	56·7	137·7	8·85	4,410	
	18	2½	31	3¼	56	4⅛	62·2	88·6	56·1	144·7	9·15	5,950	
9⅛	19	3⅞	35	0½	64	5⅛	71·35	97·95	60·95	158·9	7·85	5,950	3-cylinder simple

4-8-0 TENDER LOCOMOTIVES

TABI

Serial No.	Date	Railway or Railroad	Builder	Cylinders dia x stroke inches	Coupled Wheels diameter ft	in	Boiler Pressure lb/sq in	Grate Area sq ft	Heating Surface Firebox sq ft	Tubes sq ft	Evaporative sq ft	Superheating Surface sq ft
79	1926	TCDD	Henschel	$24\frac{3}{4} \times 26$	5	5	171	32·6	178·1†	1,780·1†	1,958·2†	688
80	1932	TCDD	Henschel & Krupp	$24\frac{3}{4} \times 26$	5	5	171	32·6	177·5†	1,766·0†	1,943·5†	73
81	1930	Beria Alta	Henschel	$16\frac{1}{2}$ & $25\frac{1}{4} \times 25\frac{5}{8}$	5	$4\frac{1}{8}$	227	42·7	201·3†	1,930·0†	2,131·3†	73
82	1947	CP	Macosa & MTM	$24\frac{3}{8} \times 26$	5	3	199	49·1	176·55†	2,178·15†	2,354·7†	62
83	1931	HNJ	Nohab	$17\frac{3}{4} \times 24$	4	$7\frac{1}{8}$	199	30	141·0†	1,398·3†	1,539·3†	57
84	1947	SJ	Nohab	$17\frac{3}{4} \times 24$	4	$7\frac{1}{8}$	199	28				
85	1932	P-O	Tours	$17\frac{3}{4}$ & $25\frac{1}{4} \times 25\frac{5}{8}$	5	$10\frac{7}{8}$	285	40·45	268·0*†	2,031·3†	2,299·3†	72
87	1940	SNCF		$17\frac{3}{4}$ & $25\frac{5}{8} \times 25\frac{5}{8}$	6	$0\frac{7}{8}$	289	40·05	268·0*†	2,021·3†	2,289·3†	73
88				17 & 24×26	6	6	100					
89		LMS		21×26	4	$8\frac{1}{2}$	190	30·5	183	1,550	1,733	36
90		SR		$16\frac{1}{2} \times 26$	5	1	200	33·0	194	1,795	1,989	37

†Fire side *Including thermic syphon

TAB

Serial No.	Date	Railway or Railroad	Builder	Cylinders dia x stroke inches	Coupled Wheels diameter ft	in	Boiler Pressure lb/sq in	Grate Area sq ft	Heating Surface Firebox sq ft	Tubes sq ft	Evaporative sq ft	Superheating Surface sq ft
94	1912	MZA	Henschel	$22\frac{7}{8} \times 26$	4	$7\frac{1}{8}$	164	41·75	150·35†	2,182·8†	2,333·15†	65
95	1912	Norte	Alsacienne	$15\frac{3}{4}$ & $24\frac{3}{8} \times 25\frac{1}{4}$	5	$1\frac{3}{8}$	227	44·1	160·3†	1,827·4†	1,987·7†	60
96	1922	Norte	Yorkshire Engine	$20\frac{1}{2} \times 26$	5	$1\frac{3}{8}$	185	50·05	198·05†	2,228·15†	2,426·2†	62
97	1914	MZA	Hanomag	$16\frac{1}{2}$ & $25\frac{1}{4} \times 25\frac{5}{8}$	5	3	221	43·05	157·8†	2,206·3†	2,364·1†	61
99	1918	MZA	MTM	$24\frac{3}{8} \times 26$	5	3	199	49·1	176·55†	2,178·15†	2,354·7†	62
100	1936	MZA	MTM	$24\frac{3}{8} \times 26$	5	3	199	49·1	176·55†	2,178·15†	2,354·7†	62
101	1920	Andaluces	Franco-Belge	22×26	5	$3\frac{3}{4}$	185	37·65	151·8†	1,513·4†	1,665·2†	48
103	1926	Andaluces	MTM	$24\frac{3}{8} \times 26$	4	$7\frac{1}{2}$	185	49·1	176·55†	2,178·15†	2,354·7†	62
105	1934	Andaluces	MTM	24×28	5	$4\frac{1}{8}$	242	56·5	194·85†	2,324·25†	2,519·1†	79
106	1922	MZyOV	Linke Hofmann	22×26	5	$1\frac{1}{2}$	171	40·9				
108	1931	Oeste	Euskalduna	22×26	5	$1\frac{1}{2}$	171	40·9	161·5†	1,451·1†	1,612·6†	47
109	1932	Oeste	Various	$24\frac{3}{8} \times 26$	5	3	199	49·1	176·55†	2,178·15†	2,354·7†	62
113	1927	C of A	Tubize	$23\frac{5}{8} \times 26$	5	$8\frac{7}{8}$						
114	1941	Renfe	MTM	24×28	5	$4\frac{1}{8}$	242	56·5	194·85†	2,324·25†	2,519·1†	79
117	1945	Renfe	Various	24×28	5	$4\frac{1}{8}$	242	56·5	194·85†	2,324·25†	2,519·1†	79
118	1950	Renfe	Various	24×28	5	$4\frac{1}{8}$	242	56·5	194·85†	2,324·25†	2,519·1†	79

†Fire side

I

Rigid in	Coupled ft	Coupled in	Engine ft	Engine in	E & T ft	E & T in	Adhesive tons	Engine tons	Tender tons	E & T tons	Fuel tons	Water gallons	Remarks
1½	19	8¼	33	1⅝	58	5⅜	63·0	86·6	50·7	137·3	6·9	4,740	
1½	19	8¼	33	1⅝			64·8	87·1	59·55	146·65	7·85	5,950	
1⅝	18	4½	32	3¾	62	11¾	57·1	84·55	53·55	138·1	6·9	5,070	4-cylinder compound
1⅞	18	8½	31	4			66·8	90·45	55·7	146·15	5·9	5,510	
	16	3	29	10⅝			50·25	72·25	41·25	113·5			3-cylinder simple
							49·2	72·85	41·3	114·15			3-cylinder simple
8¼	19	8¼	32	9¾			74·25	104·55			8·55	5,730	4-cylinder compound
8¼	19	8¼	32	9¾			77·95	107·3	56·55	163·85	9·65	7,935	4-cylinder compound
													Model ¾in to 1ft
													Scaled-up dimensions
3	17	3	28	9	52	6	62·25	81·5	42·7	124·2	5·5	3,500	Proposal. Not built
0	17	0	31	6	61	0	66	87·5	56·7	144·2	5	5,000	Proposal. Not built

I I I

Rigid in	Coupled ft	Coupled in	Engine ft	Engine in	E & T ft	E & T in	Adhesive tons	Engine tons	Tender tons	E & T tons	Fuel tons	Water gallons	Remarks
							57·1	77·3	37·4	114·7	3·95	3,195	
8¾	16	8¾	29	4¼	59	8½	60·05	77·45	49·2	126·65	7·4	4,850	4-cylinder compound
1⅞	18	8½	31	9⅞	62	1¼	61·0	86·6	50·2	136·8	6·9	4,850	3-cylinder simple
1⅞	18	8½	31	9⅞	58	3⅝	60·0	88·0	53·55	141·55	5·9	5,510	4-cylinder compound
1⅞	18	8½	31	4	58	3⅝	62·6	85·25	55·8	142·4	5·9	5,510	
1⅞	18	8½	31	4			63·0	86·1	74·8	160·9	9·85	7,495	
9½	19	2¼	31	6			49·05	66·95	29·75	96·7			
4	15	6	27	11⅝			68·8	87·85	49·2	137·05	5·9	4,410	
1⅝	20	4⅛	33	11⅜			74·8	99·4	55·3	154·7	5·9	5,510	
1⅞	16	8¾	29	4¼						111·7			
1⅞	16	8¾	29	4¼			54·1	70·7	43·1	113·8			
1⅞	18	8½	31	4	58	4⅜	66·8	90·45	55·7	146·15	5·9	5,510	
										123·4			
1⅝	20	4⅛	33	11⅜	64	7⅝	74·8	99·9	74·8	174·7	9·85	7,495	
1⅝	20	4⅛	33	11⅜						181·3			
1⅝	20	4⅛	33	11⅜			74·8	99·9	61·0	160·9	7·85	6,170	

4-8-0 TENDER LOCOMOTIVES

TABL

Serial No.	Date	Railway or Railroad	Builder	Cylinders dia x stroke inches	Coupled Wheels diameter ft in	Boiler Pressure lb/sq in	Grate Area sq ft	Heating Surface Firebox sq ft	Heating Surface Tubes sq ft	Heating Surface Evaporative sq ft	Sup heat Surf sq
119	1892	CGR	Dübs	17 x 23	3 6¼	160	17·5	98·5	911	1,009·5	—
120	1896	CGR	Neilson	17 x 23	3 6¼	160	17·5	102	976	1,078	—
125	1913	NCCR	NB	17½ x 23	3 6¾	180	17·5	119	976	1,095	—
128	1897	Soudan	Neilson	17 x 23	3 6¼	160	17·5	102	976	1,078	—
129	1905	ZASM		17 x 23	3 6¾	180	17·2	122·2	1,226	1,348·2	—
131	1907	Benguela	Avonside	17 x 23	3 6¾	160	17·5	106	939	1,045	—
132	1902	CGR	Neilson Reid	18½ x 24	4 0	180	21·35	131	1,184	1,315	—
136	1903	ZASM	NB	19 x 24	4 0	180	21	249·5[V]	1,137·8	1,387·3	—
137	1903	CGR	Neilson Reid	18½ x 24	4 0	180	27·5	125·5	1,194·0	1,319·5	—
139		SAR		17½ x 23	3 6¾	180	18·0	113	806	919	206
140		SAR		19 x 24	4 0	180	21·0	131·0	950·0	1,081·0	214
141		SAR		20 x 24	4 0	180	21·0	131·0	950·0	1,081·0	214
142	1906	CGR	Kitson	20 x 24	4 0	180	31·2	123·7	1,274·6	1,398·3	—
143	1904	NGR	NB	20½ x 24	3 9½	190	34	132	2,056	2,188	—
145		SAR	Rebuilt	19 x 27	3 9	175	21	135	1,359	1,494	—
146		SAR	Rebuilt	17 x 21	3 3	160	23·5	62	929·5	991·5	—

TABL

Serial No.	Date	Railway or Railroad	Builder	Cylinders dia x stroke inches	Coupled Wheels diameter ft in	Boiler Pressure lb/sq in	Grate Area sq ft	Heating Surface Firebox sq ft	Heating Surface Tubes sq ft	Heating Surface Evaporative sq ft	Sup heati Surf sq f
147	1901	RR	Kitson	17 x 23	3 6¾	160	17·5	102	976	1,078	—
148	1904	RR	NB	19 x 24	4 0	180	21·35	130	1,184	1,314	—
149	1910	RR	NB	19 x 24	4 0	180	21·35	141	1,184	1,325	—
150	1911	RR	NB	20 x 24	4 0	170	31·2	123	1,119	1,242	338
151	1915	RR	Montreal	20 x 24	4 0	175	32·25	123	1,162	1,285	340
152	1937	RR	Railway	20 x 24	4 0	180	36·45	167†	1,179	1,346	408·
153	1912	Shiré	Hunslet	18 x 21	3 4½	160	17·5	112	859	971	210
155	1921	TZR	Hawthorn, Leslie	18 x 21	3 4½	160	17·5	112	859	971	210
156	1930	CAR	NB	18 x 21	3 4½	160	17·5	112	859	971	210
157	1910	BCK	St Léonard	17 x 23	3 6¾	164	17·2	111·95	973·6	1,085·55	—
158	1910	Benguela	Kitson	19½ x 24	4 0	180	29·0	117	1,390	1,507	—
159	1914	Benguela	NB	20 x 24	4 0	160	35·6	135	1,122	1,257	241
160	1920	Benguela	Baldwin	20 x 24	4 0	160	18·7	133	1,302·5	1,435·5	323
161	1929	Benguela	NB	20 x 24	4 0	190	35·6	135	1,122	1,257	241
162	1923	Luanda	AW	19 x 22	3 3⅜	170	39·85	142·1	1,081·9	1,224	240
163	1923	Luanda	Henschel	19⅝ x 19⅝	3 3⅜	171	25·2	97·5	1,143·6	1,241·1	473·7

‡Fire side

K

Wheelbase				Weight in Working Order				Supplies		
Rigid in	Coupled ft in	Engine ft in	E & T ft in	Adhesive tons	Engine tons	Tender tons	E & T tons	Fuel tons	Water gallons	Remarks
0	12 0	21 3½	41 4⅜	35·05	45·5	29·0	74·5	5	2,200	
0	12 0	21 3½	46 2	35·8	46·5	32·35	78·85	5·5	2,600	
0	12 0	21 3½	46 6	39·0	49·7	39·5	89·2	6·5	2,600	
0	12 0	21 3½	42 6	36·0	46·7	34·0	80·7	5	2,600	
0	12 0	21 3½	46 2	41·9	53·3	34·1	87·4	5·5	2,600	Reboilered
0	12 0	21 3½	46 2	37·75	48·35	34·65	83·0	5·5	2,600	Wood fuel or briquettes
0	13 6	23 3	46 10½	46·6	59·05	34·0	93·05	5·5	2,730	
0	13 6	23 3	46 10½	48·7	60·6	43·05	101·7	10	3,000	ᵛDrummond water tubes in firebox
0	13 6	23 3	46 10½	46·6	59·05	36·45	95·5	10	2,855	
0	12 0	21 3½	46 2	38·0	49·1	34·1	83·2	5·5	2,600	Superheated by Railway
0	13 6	23 3	46 10½	48·0	60·75	36·45	97·2	10	2,800	Superheated by Railway
0	13 6	23 10⅝	47 6⅛	48·3	61·05	36·45	97·5	10	2,800	Superheated by Railway
0	13 6	23 4	49 2½	52·25*	65·0‖	39·7	104·7	7·5	3,000	*Also given as 49·5 ‖Also given as 63·2
6	12 9	22 6	49 0⅝	55·95	70·55	37·95	108·5	6	3,225	
4	12 6	21 4	43 0½	51·75	60·6	30·35	90·95	5·5	2,440†	†Plus 1,880 gallons in side tanks
0	11 0	19 0	44 11½	32·85	42·15	34·65	76·8	5·5	2,600**	**Plus 1,360 gallons in side tanks

A

Wheelbase				Weight in Working Order				Supplies		
Rigid in	Coupled ft in	Engine ft in	E & T ft in	Adhesive tons	Engine tons	Tender tons	E & T tons	Fuel tons	Water gallons	Remarks
0	12 0	21 3½		36·1	47·25			5	2,600	
0	13 6	23 3	46 10½	46·55	58·85	37·95	96·8	6	3,000	
0	13 6	23 3	48 4½	47·75	60·7	41·45	102·15	8·5	3,000	
0	13 6	23 4	49 10½	51·35	66·0	42·05	108·05	8·5	3,000	
0	13 6	23 4	49 10½	51·35	66·0	46·0	112·0	9·5	4,000	
0	13 6	23 4	49 10½	50·5	65·75	46·9	112·65	9·5	4,000	†Including arch tubes 150 reboilered
0	12 0	21 4	45 5⅞	34·35	46·85	31·25	78·1	3	3,000	Wood fuel
0	12 0	21 4	45 8⅞	35·25	47·95	33·45	81·4	3	3,000	Wood fuel
0	12 0	21 4	45 8⅞	36·3	49·5	39·5	89·0	7	3,000	
0	12 0	21 3½		38·4	49·2					
0	13 6	23 4	46 0	47·85	60·35	40·2	100·55	7·5	3,000	Wood fuel or briquettes
0	13 6	23 4	49 10½	51·3	66·3	42·1	108·4	5·5	3,500	Wood fuel or briquettes
0	13 6	23 4	50 1⅝	48·7	61·2	38·25	99·45	7	3,500	Wood fuel or briquettes
0	13 6	23 4	51 2½	51·75	67·65	49·0	117·65	7	4,000	Wood fuel
4	14 0	23 6		51·2	60·15	37·1	97·25	6	3,500	Wood fuel=10 tons or oil=990 gallons
2¼	13 9⅜	22 11⅝		39·35	48·9	28·05	76·95	3·9	2,645	Wood fuel=7·9 tons or oil=990 gallons

4-8-0 TENDER LOCOMOTIVES

TABL

Serial No.	Date	Railway or Railroad	Builder	Cylinders dia x stroke inches	Coupled Wheels diameter ft	in	Boiler Pressure lb/sq in	Grate Area sq ft	Heating Surface Firebox sq ft	Tubes sq ft	Evaporative sq ft	Superheat Surf sq
166	1908	Lagos	NB	17 × 23	3	$6\frac{3}{4}$	170	17·5	112	976	1,088	—
167	1934	Nigerian		19 × 22	4	0	160	17·5	112	771	883	158
168	1911	Lagos	Nasmyth, Wilson	18 × 23	3	$6\frac{1}{4}$	160	17·6	112	766	878	170
169	1933	Nigerian		18 × 23	3	$6\frac{1}{4}$	160	17·6	112	766	878	170
170	1912	Nigerian	Various	18 × 23	3	$6\frac{1}{4}$	160	17·5	112	768	880	157
171	1913	Nigerian	Various	20 × 24	3	9	160	28·5	117	1,207	1,324	314*
172	1936	Nigerian		19 × 24	3	9	180	29·4	140	1,175	1,315	228
173	1914	Nigerian	Various	17 × 21	3	4	160	15·8			952	—
174	1919	Nigerian	Beyer, Peacock	18 × 23	4	0	160	17·1	106	766	872	125
175	1923	Nigerian	Nasmyth, Wilson	18 × 23	3	$6\frac{1}{4}$	160	17·5	112	768	880	106
176	1925	Nigerian	NB	18 × 23	4	0	160	17·5	115	766	881	119
177	1909	Gold Coast	Hawthorn, Leslie	17 × 21	3	$4\frac{1}{2}$	160	16·75	97·75	963	1,060·75	—
178	1914	Gold Coast	Hawthorn, Leslie	18 × 21	3	$4\frac{1}{2}$	155	16·75	97·75	748·75	846·5	
179	1911	Sierra-Leone	Various	13 × 16	2	4	160	12·0	54	670	724	—
180	1944	Sierra-Leone	Barclay Bagnall	12 × 16	2	4	160	12·0	54	669	723	—
182	1923	Tanganyika Railway	Beyer, Peacock	18 × 23	3	7	160	18·3	129·0	956	1,085	249
183	1914	Uganda	Nasmyth, Wilson / NB	16 × 22	3	7	180	17·5	126·0	1,047	1,173	—
184	1920	Uganda	Nasmyth, Wilson	17 × 22	3	7	160	17·5	126·0	724	850	167
185	1923	Uganda	Vulcan Foundry	18 × 22	3	7	165	19·1	140·0	900	1,040	152

Wheelbase							Weight in Working Order				Supplies		
Rigid in	Coupled ft	in	Engine ft	in	E & T ft	in	Adhesive tons	Engine tons	Tender tons	E & T tons	Fuel tons	Water gallons	Remarks
0	12	0	21	$3\frac{1}{2}$	44	0	37·7	48·1	25·15	73·25	3·5	2,000	Also for Baro-Kano Railway
$10\frac{1}{2}$	13	$3\frac{3}{4}$	22	$11\frac{3}{4}$	46	$0\frac{3}{4}$	38·1	50·1	34·8	84·9	3·5	3,500	166 rebuilt by railway
0	12	0	21	$3\frac{1}{2}$	44	0	38·5	48·7	24·95	73·65	3·5	2,000	
0	12	0	21	$3\frac{1}{2}$	44	$4\frac{1}{2}$	37·5	48·95	33·6	82·55	5	3,000	168 rebuilt by railway
0	12	0	21	$3\frac{1}{2}$	44	0	38·4	50·2	27·0	77·2	5	2,000	
6	12	9	22	9	47	9	45·65	56·9	34·2	91·1	7	2,500	*Fire side. Also given as 228
6	12	9	22	9	47	9			34·2		7	2,500	171 rebuilt by railway
							31·0	41·35			3·25	2,000	
$3\frac{3}{4}$	13	$3\frac{3}{4}$	22	$11\frac{3}{4}$			37·5	50·1	31·5	81·6	3·5	3,000	
0	12	0	21	$3\frac{1}{2}$	44	$4\frac{1}{2}$	37·45	48·9	33·5	82·4	5	3,000	
$10\frac{1}{2}$	13	$3\frac{3}{4}$	22	$11\frac{3}{4}$	46	$0\frac{3}{4}$	38·0	49·85	31·9	80·75	3·5	3,000	
3	12	3	21	6	42	$2\frac{7}{8}$	32·5	42·25	25·05	67·3	3·5	2,200	
							33·65	43·65	27·4	71·05	3·5	2,200	
0	9	0	16	0	31	$1\frac{1}{4}$	17·75	22·0	10·9	32·9	1·5	1,000*	*Later tenders 1,100 galls
0	9	0	16	0	39	$1\frac{1}{4}$	19·85	24·6	19·9	44·5	4	1,665	
0	12	0	21	5			37·7	47·8	28·7	76·5	5	2,500	Wood fuel
0	12	0	21	3	45	$8\frac{5}{8}$	34·7	42·85	29·95	72·8	6	2,140	
0	12	0	21	3	42	$2\frac{3}{4}$	33·9	42·9	27·9	70·8	4·5	2,500	
3	12	3	21	5	44	$11\frac{1}{4}$	39·5	47·25	32·0	79·25	6·5	2,500	Oil fuel

4-8-0 TENDER LOCOMOTIVES

Serial No.	Date	Railway or Railroad	Builder	Cylinders dia x stroke inches	Coupled Wheels diameter ft	in	Boiler Pressure lb/sq in	Grate Area sq ft	Firebox sq ft	Tubes sq ft	Evapora-tive sq ft	Sup heat Surf sq
186	1907	Cordoba	NB	18 x 22	3	6	180	28·0	112	1,510	1,622	—
187		Cordoba		18 x 22	3	6	180	37·9	165·8	1,252·9	1,418·7	408
189	1910	BA Exhib	NB	18 & 26 x 22	3	6	180	27·75	111·7	1,510·0	1,621·7	—
190		Cia General		$17\frac{3}{8}$ x 22	3	$11\frac{1}{4}$	193					
191	1916	FCCA	NB	21 x 26	4	$7\frac{1}{2}$	160	32·5	189·0	1,557	1,746	368
192	1920	FCCA	NB	21 & 30 x 26	4	$7\frac{1}{2}$	180	32·5	182·0	1,393	1,575	247
193	1945	FCCA	NB	19 x 26	4	$7\frac{1}{2}$	225	33	189·0	1,345	1,534	358
194	1924	BAGS	Armstrong, Whitworth	$17\frac{1}{2}$ x 26	4	$7\frac{1}{2}$	200	29·25	155·0	1,732	1,887	410
195	1929	BAGS	Beyer, Peacock	$17\frac{1}{2}$ x 26	4	$7\frac{1}{2}$	200	29·2	153·0	1,732	1,885	323
196	1938	BAGS	Vulcan Foundry	$19\frac{1}{2}$ x 28	5	8	225	32·6	190·0‖	1,542	1,732‖	428
197	1949	BAGS	Vulcan Foundry	$19\frac{1}{2}$ x 28	5	8	225	32·6	189·0	1,561	1,750	347
198	1959	Roca		$17\frac{1}{2}$ x 26	4	$7\frac{1}{2}$	213					
199	1929	FCCBA	Kerr, Stuart	20 x 24	4	9	180	27·0	155·0	1,406·5	1,561·5	353
200	1931	BAW	Armstrong, Whitworth	$20\frac{1}{2}$ x 28	5	8	200	32·6	190	1,559	1,749	368
201	1946	Belgrano		⎰ $14\frac{1}{8}$ x 26 ⎱ $22\frac{7}{8}$ x 22	4	$1\frac{1}{4}$	285	42·0				

‖ Also 215 and 1,757 sq ft, four locomotives each

Serial No.	Date	Railway or Railroad	Builder	Cylinders dia x stroke inches	Coupled Wheels diameter ft	in	Boiler Pressure lb/sq in	Grate Area sq ft	Firebox sq ft	Tubes sq ft	Evapora-tive sq ft	Supe heati Surf sq
203	1896	Central of Brazil	Brooks	21 x 26	4	6	180	30·8	180	2,020	2,200	—
204	1896	Central of Brazil	Brooks	16 x 20	3	0		20·5				
205	1905	Gt Western of Brazil	NB	18 x 22	3	6	160	25·0	104	1,230	1,334	—
206	1913	Gt Western of Brazil	NB	18 x 22	3	6	160	25·0	109	980	1,089	220
208	1925	Noroeste	Henschel	$19\frac{5}{8}$ x $19\frac{5}{8}$	3	$3\frac{3}{8}$	171	27·45			1,077·5★	482·
209		Peruvian Corpn	Baldwin, Rogers	20 & 31 x 28	4	4	200					
211		Central of Peru		20 x 28	4	4	180	37·0	201·5			
212	1911	NW of Peru	NB	17 x 20	3	3	180	23·6	97	1,170	1,267	—
213	1925	Pacifico	Kitson	17 x 22	3	4	180	30·4	97	1,122	1,219	272
214	1925	Pacifico	Berlin	$17\frac{3}{4}$ x 22	3	4	180	30·4	93	1,212	1,305	374★
216	1925	Tolima	Baldwin	18 x 22	3	4	180	32·6	124	1,313	1,437	318
218	1925	Norte	Baldwin	$18\frac{1}{4}$ x 22	3	4	180	32·9	131	1,304	1,435	339
219	1927	Norte	Berlin	$18\frac{1}{8}$ x 22	3	4	180	32·5			1,429·5	392★
220	1926	Norte	Haine St Pierre	$18\frac{1}{4}$ x 22	3	4	180	32·85	115	1,313	1,428	331
223		Pacifico	Skoda	18 x 22	3	4	180	32·4	120·0	1,307·4	1,427·4	327·2
226	1928	Dorada	Hawthorn, Leslie	17 x 22	3	4	180	30·4	97	1,120	1,217	272

★Fire side

I

Rigid in	Coupled ft	Coupled in	Engine ft	Engine in	E & T ft	E & T in	Adhesive tons	Engine tons	Tender tons	E & T tons	Fuel tons	Water gallons	Remarks
0	12	0	22	8	46	8½	42·65	54·7	33·7	88·4	240*	3,000	*Cubic feet; wood fuel. Metre gauge
0	12	0	22	8	46	8½	41·25	52·85	40·25	93·1	172*	3,020	*Cubic feet; wood fuel. Rebuild of 186
0	12	0	22	8	48	0	42·5	55·05	34·25	89·3	4	3,000	2-cylinder compound. Metre gauge
								64·85	42·3	107·15	7·4	3,900	Metre gauge
0½	16	0½	28	5¼	57	0⅝	59·2	77·45	60·2	137·65	5·75	6,000	†Fire side. Broad gauge
0½	16	0½	28	5¼	57	0⅝	60·75	80·05	67·0	147·05	7‡	6,000	2-cylinder compound. Broad gauge
0½	16	0½	28	5¼	57	1	62·8	82·1	66·05	148·15	7·25‡	6,000	‡Oil fuel. Broad gauge
5	17	6	28	9½	55	1½	63·9	83·7	51·35	135·05	8·75‡	4,000	‡Oil fuel. 3-cylinder simple. Broad gauge
5	17	6	28	9½	59	4½	66·4	85·5	65·4	150·9	11·5‡	5,500	‡Oil fuel. 3-cylinder simple. Broad gauge
6	18	6	30	7	60	10¾	64·35	88·1	67·2	155·3	11·0‡	6,000	‡Oil fuel. Broad gauge
6	18	6	30	4	60	7¾	61·8	82·35	66·1	148·45	11·6‡	6,000	‡Oil fuel. Broad gauge
5	17	6	28	9½			63·95	83·65					Rebuild of 194 and 195
5	16	5	27	9	50	9	48·4	64·0	34·65	98·65	5	3,000	Standard gauge
6	18	6	30	5	55	10½	60·65	82·65	63·15	145·8	11·25‡	5,750	‡Oil fuel. Broad gauge
							54	68					4-cylinder compound. Metre gauge. Rebuilt by Railway Works

I I

Rigid in	Coupled ft	Coupled in	Engine ft	Engine in	E & T ft	E & T in	Adhesive tons	Engine tons	Tender tons	E & T tons	Fuel tons	Water gallons	Remarks
6	15	6	25	3			63·4	75·9	36·6	112·5			Broad gauge
							35·7	43·75	30·35	74·1			Metre gauge
11	11	10½	21	7½	41	6	35·25	46·2	25·3	71·5	3·75	2,000	Metre gauge
11	11	10½	21	7½	41	6	37·1	49·0	25·7	74·7	3·75	2,000	Metre gauge
2¼			22	11⅝	47	4⅛	38·4	48·4	28·55	76·95	3·95	2,645	Wood fuel. Metre gauge
								60					2-cylinder compound Standard gauge
6	14	3							40·3		1,230†	4,000	†Gallons of oil. Standard gauge. Rebuilt by Railway
2			19	9	46	1	38·2	47·0	30·95	77·95	5	2,500	3ft gauge
9	12	0	21	4	46	0	40·85	49·55	29·9	79·45	5·35	2,750	3ft gauge
6½‡	12	0½	21	3⅞			43·1	52·85	30·8	83·65	5·3	2,755	‡Changed to 3ft 9¼in. 3ft gauge
11	12	6	21	11	47	4¾	46·0	57·1	31·9	89·0	5·3	2,750	3ft gauge
11	12	6	21	11	47	7	47·8	57·2	31·45	88·65	5·35	2,750	Two were oil burners. Metre gauge
11	12	6	21	11	47	8¾	47·25	57·45	31·7	89·15	5·3	2,755	Metre gauge
11	12	6	21	11			47·7	57·55					Metre gauge
11	12	6	21	11	47	7⅞	44·0	53·45	30·9	84·35	5·35	2,755	3ft gauge
9	12	0	21	4	46	0	40·9	49·65	31·9	81·55	1,200†	2,750	†Gallons of oil. 3ft gauge

4-8-0 TENDER LOCOMOTIVES

Serial No.	Date	Railway or Railroad	Builder	Cylinders dia x stroke inches	Coupled Wheels diameter ft	in	Boiler Pressure lb/sq in	Grate Area sq ft	Heating Surface Firebox sq ft	Tubes sq ft	Evaporative sq ft	Sup heat Surf sq
228	1899	NZGR	Sharp, Stewart	16 × 22	3	6½	175	17·5	101·3	939	1,040·3	—
229	1901	NZGR	Addington	16 × 22	3	6½	175	17·3	98	939	1,037	—
231	1911	NZGR	Addington	16 × 22	3	6½	175	16·7	101†	687†	788†	206
232	1928	NZGR		16 × 22	3	6½	200	26·4				
233	1915	NZGR	Price	17 × 22	3	6½	175	16·8	109	625	734	432
234	1900	Emu Bay	Dübs	17½ × 22	3	9	175	16·0	112·75	1,072·4	1,185·15	—
235	1927	TGR		16½ × 22	3	7	160	17·3	106	750	856	185
							†Some locomotives		102·5	610	712·5	293·

Serial No.	Date	Railway or Railroad	Builder	Cylinders dia x stroke inches	Coupled Wheels diameter ft	in	Boiler Pressure lb/sq in	Grate Area sq ft	Heating Surface Firebox sq ft	Tubes sq ft	Evaporative sq ft	Sup heat Surf sq
236	1901	WAGR	Dübs	17 × 23	3	6½	175	18·9	127	1,267	1,394	—
237	1912	WAGR	NB	19 × 23	3	6½	160	18·8	125	977	1,102	261
238	1920	MRWA	Baldwin	18 × 23	3	9	160	17·0	124·6	882·5	1,007·1	284
239	1903	SAR	Islington	16½ × 22	3	7	185	17·3	109	939	1,048	—
241	1922	SAR	Martin Walkers	16½ × 22	3	7	185	17·3	109	665	774	136
242	1903	QR	Ipswich	16 × 22	3	9	175	18·5	107	895	1,002	—
243	1913	QR	Various	16½ × 22	3	9	170	18·5	116	706·4	822	178
244	1914	QR	Ipswich	18 × 23	4	0	175	21·35	147·25	1,192·75	1,340·0	
245	1914	QR	Ipswich	18 × 23	4	0	170	21·35	147·25	896	1,043·25	225
247	1919	QR	Ipswich	17 × 22	3	9	160	18·5	116	657·4	773·4	195
248	1947	QR	Walkers	17 × 22	3	9	175	18·5	116	647·4	763·4	195
249	1927	QR	Armstrong, Whitworth	17 × 22	3	9		18·5	116	682·1	798·1	177
251	1922	QR	Ipswich	19 × 23	4	0	160	21·35	147·25	896·0	1,043·25	225
252	1934	QR	Walkers	19 × 23	4	0	160	21·35	147·35	866·85	1,014·2	192
253	1924	CR	Thompson	17 × 22	3	9	160	18·5	116·0	706·8*	822·8*	177

Serial No.	Date	Railway or Railroad	Builder	Cylinders dia x stroke inches	Coupled Wheels diameter ft	in	Boiler Pressure lb/sq in	Grate Area sq ft	Heating Surface Firebox sq ft	Tubes sq ft	Evaporative sq ft	Sup heat Surf sq
254	1903			16 × 22	3	7	180	17·5	126·2	1,164·8	1,291·0	—
255	1904	EBR	NB	16 × 22	3	6½	180	17·5	126·2	1,164·8	1,291·0	—
256	1906	ABR	NB	16 × 22	3	7	180	17·5	126	1,166	1,292	—
258	1907	SMR	NB	16 × 22	3	7	180	17·5	126	1,166	1,292	—
262	1914	Nizam's	Nasmyth, Wilson	16 × 22	3	7	180	17·5	126	1,047	1,173	—
264	1916	M & SMR	NB	17 × 22	3	7	160	16·8	125	726	851	160
267	1923	Nizam's	Nasmyth, Wilson	17 × 22	3	7	160	17·5	126	782	908	153
269	1925	M & SMR	Bagnall	17 × 22	3	7	160	16·8	124	785	909	150
270	1928	BDR	Nasmyth, Wilson	17 × 22	3	7	160	17·5	126	782	908	153
271	1936	JDR	Rheinmetal	17 × 22	3	7	160			785		
274	1925	Bhavnagar	Hanomag	12 × 16	2	4		12			724	—
275	1935	Bhavnagar	Bagnall	12 × 16	2	4	160	12	54	635	689	—
276	1911	Ceylon	Kitson	21 × 24	3	7	160	40	180			
277	1913	Ceylon	Kitson	21 × 24	3	7	160	42·5	188	1,829	2,017	424
278	1928	Ceylon	Hunslet	17 × 22	4	0	170	23·5	117·5	859	976·5	201
279	1951	Ceylon	Bagnall	17 × 22	4	0	180	23·5	126	854	980	201
280	1933	HKR	Hunslet	16⅛ × 21⅝	3	8⅛	200	19·4	102	769	871	376

III

	Wheelbase				Weight in Working Order				Supplies		
igid in	Coupled ft in	Engine ft in	E & T ft in	Adhesive tons	Engine tons	Tender tons	E & T tons	Fuel tons	Water gallons	Remarks
0*	13 6	23 6	44 9⅛	31·65	42·15	21·95	64·1	2·75	1,700	*Changed to 13ft 6in
6	13 6	23 6	45 0½	31·75	43·0	25·5	68·5	4	1,700	
4	12 4	22 8½	44 10	32·3	43·9	25·5	69·4	4	1,700	
4	12 4	22 8½			44·1	22·7	66·8			231 rebuilt
4	12 4	22 4	45 2½	32·7	43·35	25·0	68·35	4	1,700	
4	12 6	22 0½	43 8½	37·55	47·55	28·15	75·7	3·5	2,000	
0	13 6	23 6	46 0½	30·75	41·25	32·0	73·25	6	2,500	240 rebuilt by TGR

IV

	Wheelbase				Weight in Working Order				Supplies		
igid in	Coupled ft in	Engine ft in	E & T ft in	Adhesive tons	Engine tons	Tender tons	E & T tons	Fuel tons	Water gallons	Remarks
6	12 6	22 11	46 5½	42·9	53·35	28·1	81·45	4·5	2,200	
6	12 6	22 11	46 11¾	42·7	55·35	30·6	85·95	5·5	2,200	
6	12 9	22 0½	46 0½	36	48·15	30·7	78·85	5	2,500	
6	13 6	23 6	46 8	30·75	41·25	32·0	73·25	6	2,500	Later superheated, same boiler as 241
0	13 6	23 6	46 6	34·6	44·8	35·0	79·8	8	2,500	240 rebuilt by Railway
6	12 6	21 6	44 11½	30·9	40·95	32·0	72·95	4·5	3,000	
6	12 6	21 6	45 0	33·15	44·0	36·9	80·9	8	3,000	
6	12 6	22 1	48 4¾	40·4	52·65	40·0	92·65	7	3,500	
6	12 6	22 1	48 4¾	40·0	53·0	40·0	93·0	7	3,500	
6	12 6	21 6	45 0	33·1	44·85	33·5	78·35	4·5	3,050	
6	12 6	21 6	45 0	35·55	48·05	34·85	82·9	5·25	3,050	
6	12 6	21 6	45 0	33·85			78·25	4·5	3,000	
6	12 6	22 0	48 4¾	41·7	54·25	40·15	94·4	7	3,500	
6	12 6	22 1	48 4¾	40·0	52·9	44·1	97·0	11	3,500	
6	12 6	21 6	45 0	33·1	44·85	33·4†	78·25†	4·5†	3,000	*Later 647·4 and 763·4sq ft
					†Later	35·4	80·25	6·5		

V

	Wheelbase				Weight in Working Order				Supplies		
Rigid ft in	Coupled ft in	Engine ft in	E & T ft in	Adhesive tons	Engine tons	Tender tons	E & T tons	Fuel tons	Water gallons	Remarks
9 6	14 3	23 4½	44 10¾	32*	39·5*	22·95	62·45*	4	2,000	Standard design
9 6	14 3	23 4½	44 10½	31·85	39·55	22·95	62·3	4	2,000	
8 0	12 0	21 3	46 3	32·15	40·05	25·0	65·05	3	2,000	
2 0	12 0	20 6	42 3¼	34·0	41·0	22·55	63·55	4·5	1,600	Wood fuel
	12 0	21 3	42 2¾	32·4	41·4	27·8	69·2	4·5	2,500	
2 0	12 0	20 6	42 2¾	33·3	41·75	29·05	70·8	4·5	2,650	
	12 0	21 3	42 2¾	32·6	41·4	28·0	69·4	4·5	2,500	
2 0	12 0	20 0	42 2¾	33·5	41·75	28·75	70·5	4·5	2,650	
	12 0	21 3	41 2⅛	32·0	42·05	22·6	64·65	6	1,500	
	12 0	21 3	42 3¼	32·65	41·5	23·2	64·7	4	2,000	
		16 0	31 1¼	19·0	23·7	11·45	35·15	1·5	1,100	
	9 0	16 0	31 4¼		24·5	13·25	37·75	3	1,100	
8 0	12 0	22 0	49 0½	62·0	77·2	40·4	117·6	5	3,000	
8 0	12 0	22 0	49 10	62·4	76·55	40·4	116·95	5	3,000	
4 0	14 0	23 8½	48 3½	36·0	49·4	35·45	84·85	4	2,700	
4 0	14 0	23 8½	48 2	35·75	49·0	36·6	85·6	4	2,700	
	12 9½	22 0¼	45 3¾	32·7	44·9	31·55	76·45	3·95	2,640	

*Estimated weights

INDEX

4-8-0 TENDER LOCOMOTIVES